Printed at the Mathematical Centre, 49, 2e Boerhaavestraat, Amsterdam.

The Mathematical Centre, founded the 11-th of February 1946, is a non-profit institution aiming at the promotion of pure mathematics and its applications. It is sponsored by the Netherlands Government through the Netherlands Organization for the Advancement of Pure Research (Z.W.O), by the Municipality of Amsterdam, by the University of Amsterdam, by the Free University at Amsterdam, and by industries.

MATHEMATICAL CENTRE TRACTS

H.A. LAUWERIER

ASYMPTOTIC ANALYSIS

MATHEMATISCH CENTRUM   AMSTERDAM 1974

AMS (MOS) subject classification scheme 41A60 (41.50), 33-XX (33)

ISBN 90 6196 098 3

CONTENTS

PREFACE

This tract contains the expanded lecture notes of courses on asymptotic methods in applied analysis given for students in mathematical physics
at the University of Amsterdam. In this volume we consider the asymptotic
behaviour of real and complex functions which are explicitly given by an
integral expression. The treatment of the asymptotic behaviour of functions
which are implicitly determined by a differential equation will be given
in a second volume which will also contain an exposition of the important
techniques of regular and singular perturbation.

Asymptotics is an art that can be mastered only by studying a great
number of special cases rather than using general theorems. The author
therefore has attempted to illustrate the techniques of asymptotic analysis by a great variety of worked-out examples.

Much attention is given to the asymptotic expansion of functions which
can be expressed as a Laplace integral or more generally as an integral to
which the saddle point technique can be applied. A number of special functions such as Bessel functions and confluent hypergeometric functions are
treated in this way.

A few topics are included here which are not usually found in the
text-books. We mention in particular the chapters on factorial series, the
Euler transformation, the asymptotic behaviour of Cauchy integrals and
asymptotics in the theory of probability. Also much original material is
included.

The text is aimed at students in analysis and in mathematical physics.
The style may be reminiscent of the lecture room. In general the systematic
treatment and the theorems are preceded or followed by examples and special
cases. Some theorems could easily be generalized and conditions may be re-
laxed somewhat. However, for the sake of simplicity and clearness the
theorems are sometimes stated in a simple and special form. Obvious gene-
ralizations are left to the reader.

H.A.L.

1. INTRODUCTION

In asymptotics we consider the behaviour of a function f of a variable z when z tends to a specific value z_0. Following the conventions of current practice we take either $z_0 = \infty$ or $z_0 = 0$. However, both cases are entirely equivalent since z can be replaced by z^{-1}. If the independent variable is real and runs through all positive real numbers to infinity, we denote it by ω. If ω is restricted to the natural numbers, we shall usually write n instead of ω. It is convenient to take $z_0 = 0$ for asymptotics with respect to a complex variable z.

Sometimes f depends also on a further variable, say a parameter λ. Then asymptotic properties may be formulated either for specific values of λ or uniformly for some set Λ of λ-values.

The Landau symbols

There are the following two symbols O and o introduced by Landau for describing order relations between asymptotic expressions. For $\omega \to \infty$ their meaning is explained as follows.

$$(1.1) \qquad f(\omega) = O(g(\omega))$$

means that there exist constants c and ω_0 such that

$$(1.2) \qquad |f(\omega)| < c|g(\omega)| \text{ for } \omega > \omega_0.$$

The order relation

$$(1.3) \qquad f(\omega) = o(g(\omega))$$

is simply another way of saying that

$$(1.4) \qquad f(\omega) / g(\omega) \to 0 \text{ for } \omega \to \infty.$$

The relation $f = o(g)$ says that f is of order less than g. The relation $f = O(g)$ says that f is of order less or equal than g. Thus $f = o(g)$ implies $f = O(g)$.
The order relations may hold uniformly in some set Λ if f and g depend on λ. For (1.2) this means that the constant c is independent of λ.

Sometimes the symbol ~ is used to express asymptotic equivalence between non-vanishing functions f and g. Then

(1.5) $f(\omega) \sim g(\omega)$

means that

(1.6) $\lim f(\omega) / g(\omega) = 1.$

Example 1.1

a.   Stirling's formula

$$n! \sim n^{n+1/2} e^{-n} \sqrt{2\pi}.$$

b.   Wallis' formula

$$2^{-2n}\binom{2n}{n} = \frac{1.3.5\ldots (2n-1)}{2.4.6\ldots 2n} \sim \sqrt{\frac{1}{n\pi}}.$$

c.   The following asymptotic expressions of the same function give an increasing amount of information.

$$(n^2+n+1)^{1/2} = O(n),$$
$$(n^2+n+1)^{1/2} \sim n,$$
$$(n^2+n+1)^{1/2} = n + O(1),$$
$$(n^2+n+1)^{1/2} = n + \frac{1}{2} + o(1),$$
$$(n^2+n+1)^{1/2} = n + \frac{1}{2} + O(n^{-1}).$$

d.   Euler's constant $\gamma = .5772\ldots\ldots\ldots$.

$$1 + \frac{1}{2} + \frac{1}{3} + \ldots + \frac{1}{n} \sim \log n,$$
$$1 + \frac{1}{2} + \frac{1}{3} + \ldots + \frac{1}{n} = \log n + \gamma + o(1),$$
$$1 + \frac{1}{2} + \frac{1}{3} + \ldots + \frac{1}{n} = \log n + \gamma + O(n^{-1}),$$
$$1 + \frac{1}{2} + \frac{1}{3} + \ldots + \frac{1}{n} = \log n + \gamma + (2n)^{-1} + o(n^{-1}).$$

Definition 1.1

A sequence of functions $\{\phi_k(\omega)\}$ is said to be an *asymptotic sequence* (AS) as $\omega \to \infty$ if for all k

(1.7) $\qquad \phi_{k+1} = o(\phi_k)$ for $\omega \to \infty$.

Such an AS is formed for example by successive negative powers of ω

(1.8) $\qquad 1, \omega^{-1}, \omega^{-2}, \omega^{-3}, \ldots$.

A slightly more general AS is given by $\phi_k = \omega^{-\lambda_k}$ with $\lambda_k \to \infty$ and $\lambda_1 < \lambda_2 < \lambda_3 < \ldots$.

Definition 1.2

The function f is said to have an *asymptotic expansion* (AE) of order N with respect to the AS $\{\phi_k\}$ if there exist constants a_k such that

(1.9) $\qquad f = \sum_{k=0}^{N} a_k \phi_k + o(\phi_N)$.

It is clear that an AE of order N is an AE for all lower orders. The constants a_k can be determined by means of

(1.10) $\qquad a_k = \lim_{\omega \to \infty} (f - \sum_{j=0}^{k-1} a_j \phi_j)/\phi_k$.

This shows that an AE of a given function is unique. On the other hand we shall soon see that more functions can have the same AE.
In many cases it is possible to construct an infinite AE. Then we simply write

(1.11) $\qquad f \sim \sum a_k \phi_k$

which means that (1.9) is true for all N.

If with respect to a given AS a function g has an AE (1.11) with zero coefficients, it is said to be asymptotically zero (notation $g \sim 0$) with respect to that sequence. According to (1.10) this means that

(1.12) $\qquad g / \phi_k \to 0$ for all k.

If $f \sim \sum a_k \phi_k$ and $g \sim \sum b_k \phi_k$, it follows easily from (1.10) that the linear combination $\alpha f + \beta g$ has the AE $\sum(\alpha a_k + \beta b_k)\phi_k$. If g is asymptotically zero, then f and f + g have the same AE.

Example 1.2

The following statements hold for the AS $\{\omega^{-k}\}$.

a. $\qquad (\omega+1)^{-1} \sim \sum_{k=1} (-1)^{k-1} \omega^{-k}.$

b. $\qquad \int_0^\infty (t+\omega)^{-1} e^{-t} dt \sim \sum_{k=1} (-1)^{k-1}(k-1)! \omega^{-k}.$

c.   The functions $e^{-\omega}$, $\omega^{-\log \omega}$, $\omega^{-\omega}$ are asymptotically zero.

2. ASYMPTOTIC POWER SERIES

We consider the asymptotic behaviour of a function f for $\omega \to \infty$ with respect to the AS $\{\omega^{-k}\}$. The resulting AE

$$(2.1) \qquad f \sim \sum a_k \omega^{-k}$$

is called an asymptotic power series (APS).
We shall, however, change the notation a little bit by writing $x = \omega^{-1}$ and using x (x > 0) instead of ω. If the remainder of the n-th order APS is defined as

$$(2.2) \qquad R_N(x) = f(x) - \sum_{k=0}^{N} a_k x^k ,$$

then the full APS

$$(2.3) \qquad f(x) \sim \sum_{k=0} a_k x^k$$

implies that not only

$$(2.4) \qquad R_N(x) = o(x^N),$$

but that even better

$$(2.5) \qquad R_N(x) = O(x^{N+1}).$$

We mention the following few theorems the proofs of which depend on simple straightforward analysis.

Theorem 2.1

If $f \sim \sum a_k x^k$ and $g \sim \sum b_k x^k$, then fg has the APS which is obtained by the formal multiplication of the corresponding series.

Theorem 2.2

If $f \sim \sum a_k x^k$ and $a_0 \neq 0$, then f^{-1} has the APS which is obtained by the corresponding formal procedure.

6

Theorem 2.3

If $f \sim \sum_k a_k x^k$, then

(2.6) $$\int_0^x f(t)dt \sim \sum_{k=0} \frac{a_k}{k+1} x^{k+1},$$

and

(2.7) $$\int_0^x \frac{f(t) - a_0}{t} dt \sim \sum_{k=1} \frac{a_k}{k} x^k.$$

Theorem 2.4

If $f(x)$ has a continuous derivative and if $f'(x)$ possesses an APS then the latter can be obtained by formal differentiation of the APS of $f(x)$

(2.8) $$f' \sim \sum_{k=1} k a_k x^{k-1}.$$

If $f(x)$ is repeatedly differentiable and admits a convergent Taylor series

(2.9) $$f(x) = \sum_{k=0}^{\infty} \frac{1}{k!} f^{(k)}(0)x^k, \quad |x| < R,$$

then it is almost obvious that this is also the APS of $f(x)$.
However, it comes somewhat as a surprise that the same result also holds for a formal Taylor series which need not be convergent.
In fact we have the following property.

Theorem 2.5

If $f(x)$ is repeatedly differentiable in an interval $0 \leq x \leq a$, then the formal Taylor series represented by the right-hand side of (2.9) is the APS of $f(x)$.

(2.10) $$f(x) \sim \sum_{k=0} \frac{1}{k!} f^{(k)}(0)x^k.$$

Proof

The remainder of the finite Taylor expansion can be written as

$$R_N(x) = \frac{1}{N!} \int_0^x (x-t)^N f^{(N+1)}(t)dt.$$

If f belongs to some class $C^m(0,a)$, then for $N+1 \le m$ we have the following estimate

$$|R_N(x)| \le c \int_0^x (x-t)^N dt$$

so that

$$R_N(x) = 0(x^{N+1}).$$

From a given APS other asymptotic expansions can be derived in a variety of ways. A few simple ways are shown in the preceding theorems. A more interesting method is offered by Laplace transformation. If

$$g(\omega) = \int_0^\infty e^{-\omega x} f(x)dx$$

is the Laplace transform of $f(x)$ and if $f \sim \sum a_k x^k$, then formal transformation gives the following APS

$$g(\omega) \sim \sum_{k=0} k! \, a_k \omega^{-k-1}.$$

The full discussion will be postponed to a later chapter. Here we restrict ourselves to the following simple theorem.

Theorem 2.6

Let $f(x)$ be continuous for $0 \le x \le a$ and have the APS $\sum a_k x^k$. Then

(2.11) $$\int_0^a e^{-\omega x} f(x)dx \sim \sum_{k=0} k! \, a_k \omega^{-k-1} \quad \text{as } \omega \to \infty.$$

Proof

We write $f(x) = \sum_{k=0}^N a_k x^k + R_N(x)$. The corresponding remainder of the transformed APS can be written as

$$S_N(\omega) = \int_0^a e^{-\omega x} R_N(x)dx - \sum_{k=0}^N a_k \int_a^\infty e^{-\omega x} x^k dx.$$

We have to show that $\omega^{N+1}S_N(\omega) \to 0$ for all N. Since $|R_N(x)| < cx^{N+1}$, we have

$$\left| \int_0^a e^{-\omega x}R_N(x)dx \right| < c \int_0^\infty e^{-\omega x}x^{N+1}dx = O(\omega^{-N-2}).$$

Further, it is easy to show that

$$\omega^{-N-1} \int_a^\infty e^{-\omega x}x^k dx \to 0$$

for all k.

Example 2.1

a.   The coefficients of the Taylor expansion of exp - 1/x are all zero. This means that the Taylor series converges but does not represent the function. However, it is true according to theorem 2.5 that the Taylor series is the right APS. Thus exp - 1/x is asymptotically zero as $x \to +0$.

b.   We consider the function

$$f(x) = \int_0^\infty \frac{e^{-t}}{1+tx}\, dt, \quad x \geq 0.$$

A simple calculation shows that $f^{(k)}(0) = (-1)^k k!k!$. The formal Taylor series becomes $\sum(-1)^k k!x^k$ which, however, diverges for all $x \neq 0$. Yet it is the APS of $f(x)$.

Example 2.2

Starting from the Taylor series and APS

$$(1+x)^{-1} = \sum_{k=0}^{\infty} (-1)^k x^k$$

we obtain by using (2.10) for $a = \infty$

$$\int_0^\infty \frac{e^{-\omega x}}{1+x}\, dx \sim \sum_{k=0}^{\infty} \frac{(-1)^k k!}{\omega^{k+1}}.$$

From theorem 2.5 it is clear that a power series with a non-vanishing radius of convergence is the APS of its sum. However, the preceding examples show that an APS may diverge for all $x \neq 0$. But the following theorem shows that also to a divergent power series a function can be associated for which this series is its APS. Of course this association is not unique since to this function an arbitrary asymptotically vanishing function may be added.

Theorem 2.7

For any formal power series $\sum_{k=0}^{\infty} a_k x^k$ there exists a function f(x) with this series as its APS. It is possible to find such a function which is infinitely differentiable in a given interval (0,a).

Proof

Take a = 1 and define

$$(2.12) \qquad f(x) = \sum_{k=0}^{\infty} a_k (1 - \exp - \frac{\phi(x)}{|a_k|}) x^k,$$

where $\phi(x)$ is some positive function of x.

Since $1 - e^{-a} \le a$ for $a \ge 0$, the terms of this series are dominated by $x^k \phi(x)$ so that f(x) converges for $0 \le x < 1$. We have

$$\left| f(x) - \sum_{k=0}^{N} a_k x^k \right| \le \sum_{k=0}^{N} |a_k| x^k \exp - \frac{\phi(x)}{|a_k|} + \phi(x) \sum_{k=N+1}^{\infty} x^k.$$

If $\phi(x) = x^{-1/2}$ the terms of the first series on the right-hand side are all asymptotically zero. The second series is $O(x^{N+1/2})$ so that the left-hand side is certainly $o(x^N)$. Since this is true for all N, the series $\sum a_k x^k$ is the APS of f(x).

3. ANALYTIC FUNCTIONS

The asymptotic properties of a complex function f of the complex variable $z = x+iy$ or $z = r \exp i\theta$ when $z \to 0$ or $z \to \infty$ may depend on the phase θ. Order relations such as $f = 0(g)$ may be uniformly valid in some sector $\alpha \leq \theta \leq \beta$ but may loose their validity outside this sector.

Example 3.1

For $z \to 0$ the asymptotic relation $\exp - 1/z \sim 0$ with respect to any power series of z holds uniformly within any closed sector contained in the domain $-\frac{1}{2}\pi < \theta < \frac{1}{2}\pi$. However, for purely imaginary z we have $|\exp - 1/z| = 1$. Hence the relation above does not hold uniformly in the domain $-\frac{1}{2}\pi < \theta < \frac{1}{2}\pi$. For $\frac{1}{2}\pi \leq |\theta| \leq \pi$ things are even worse.

As a rule we consider only asymptotic relations with respect to $z \to 0$. Then a suitable asymptotic sequence is formed by successive powers of z such as $\{z^k\}$ or more generally $\{z^{\lambda_k}\}$ as in the real case. We repeat that an asymptotic expansion such as

$$(3.1) \qquad f(z) \sim \sum_{k=0}^{\infty} a_k z^k$$

means that for each index N there exist a positive constant c_N and a small number ε such that

$$(3.2) \qquad \left| f(z) - \sum_{k=0}^{N} a_k z^k \right| < c_N |z|^{N+1} \text{ for } |z| < \varepsilon.$$

Of course the coefficients a_k and the constants c_N may depend on the phase of z. If, however, for some sector $\alpha \leq \theta \leq \beta$ it is always possible to find a constant c_N independent of θ, the expansion is called a uniform asymptotic power series (UAPS).

From now on we consider only asymptotic expansions which are holomorphic in a fan-shaped region $\alpha < \theta < \beta$, $a < r < b$. As a rule in applications we have either $a = 0$ or $b = \infty$ but since by using the transformation $z \to z^{-1}$ asymptotics with respect to $z = \infty$ may be reduced to that for $z = 0$, it suffices to take $a = 0$. As a rule an expansion like (3.1) holds uniformly in some sector with coefficients independent of θ. However, in different sectors the analytic function may possess different expansions, an effect which is known as the Stokes' phenomenon.

The situation is particularly simple for an analytic function which is holomorphic at $z = 0$.

Theorem 3.1

If $f(z)$ is holomorhic for $|z| \leq R$ then its Taylor series is a UAPS.

Proof

For $|z| < R$ we write

$$f(z) = \sum_{k=0}^{N} a_k z^k + \frac{z^{N+1}}{2\pi i} \oint_{|\zeta|=R} \frac{f(\zeta)}{(\zeta-z)\zeta^{N+1}} \, d\zeta.$$

The remainder is in absolute value less than

$$\frac{M|z|^{N+1}}{(R-|z|)R^N} \, ,$$

where M is the maximum value of $|f(\zeta)|$ on the circle $|\zeta| = R$. Thus for each N the relation (3.2) holds uniformly irrespectively the phase of z.

If $f(z)$ possesses an essential singularity at $z = 0$ the Stokes phenomenon may be exhibited.

Example 3.2

For $f(z) = \frac{1}{2}(e^z + e^{-z} \tanh z^{-1})$ we have the following asymptotic expansions

$$f(z) \sim \cosh z \sim \sum_{k=0}^{\infty} \frac{z^{2k}}{(2k)!} \quad \text{for Re } z > 0,$$

$$f(z) \sim \sinh z \sim \sum_{k=0}^{\infty} \frac{z^{2k+1}}{(2k+1)!} \quad \text{for Re } z < 0.$$

The theorems of the preceding section also hold for the APS of analytic functions. In particular the theorems 2.1, 2.2 and 2.3 are valid with obvious modifications if the expansions are uniform in some sector. However, theorem 2.4 can be replaced by the following theorem.

Theorem 3.2

If $f(z)$ is holomorphic in $\alpha < \theta < \beta$, $0 < r < b$ and if

$$f(z) \sim \sum_{k=0} a_k z^k \qquad \text{uniformly in } \theta,$$

then

$$f'(z) \sim \sum_{k=1} k a_k z^{k-1}$$

uniformly in any smaller sector $\alpha < \alpha_1 < \theta < \beta_1 < \beta$.

Proof

We write $f(z) = \sum_{k=0}^{N} a_k z^k + z^{N+1} g(z)$, where $|g(z)| < c$ in the given sector.

Since $f'(z) = \sum_{k=1}^{N} k a_k z^{k-1} + z^N \{(N+1)g(z) + zg'(z)\}$, it suffices to show

that $zg'(z)$ is uniformly bounded in a smaller sector.

However, this can easily be deduced from the representation

$$zg'(z) = \frac{z}{2\pi i} \oint \frac{g(\zeta)}{(\zeta-z)^2} \, d\zeta$$

where the path of integration is an Apollonius circle $|\zeta-z| = \delta|\zeta|$ where δ is a sufficiently small positive number.

A UAPS of an analytic function may not exist but, if it does exist, it is unique. On the other hand many analytic functions may have the same UAPS for some sector $-\alpha < \theta < \alpha$, where for simplicity the sector is chosen symmetric with respect to the positive real axis $\theta = 0$. This result follows from the simple observation that the function $\exp(-z^{-\gamma})$, where γ is a positive real number, vanishes asymptotically with respect to all powers of z in the sector $|\theta| < \frac{1}{2}\pi/\gamma$. Hence, for $\gamma < \frac{1}{2}\pi/\alpha$ this function is uniformly asymptotically zero in the given sector.

We shall now consider the interesting problem whether a given formal power series $\sum a_k z^k$ can be the APS of some analytic function. If the series converges within some circle there is no difficulty since the power series is the Taylor series of the analytic function it represents and theorem 4.1 can be applied. But, if the series diverges it is not immediately clear whether an analytic function can be constructed for which the given series is its APS. Yet the answer is still in the affirmative. We have even the following theorem.

Theorem 3.3

Is $\sum\limits_{k=0} a_k z^k$ a formal power series and S a sector $|\arg z| < \gamma$, $|z| < R$, then there exists an analytic function holomorphic in S for which the given series is its UAPS in S.

Proof

We consider the function

$$f(z) = \sum_{k=0}^{\infty} (1 - \exp - \frac{1}{|a_k| z^\alpha}) a_k z^k$$

with $0 < \alpha < \min(\tfrac{1}{2}\pi/\gamma, 1)$.

Making use of the inequality

$$|1 - e^{-z}| \leq |z|, \; \text{Re } z \geq 0,$$

which is proved below as a separate lemma, it easily follows that $f(z)$ converges for $|z| < 1$, $|\arg z| \leq \gamma$ and is holomorphic. We shall now show that $f(z)$ has the UAPS $\sum\limits_{k=0} a_k z^k$. The remainder may be estimated as

$$|R_N(z)| = |f(z) - \sum_{k=0}^{N} a_k z^k| \leq \sum_{k=0}^{N} |a_k| \exp(-\frac{1}{|a_k| x^\alpha}) |z|^k +$$

$$+ \sum_{k=N+1}^{\infty} |1 - \exp - \frac{1}{|a_k| z^\alpha}| \; |a_k| |z|^k \leq$$

$$\leq \frac{A}{1-|z|} \exp - \frac{1}{A x^\alpha} + \frac{|z|^{N+1-\alpha}}{1-|z|}, \; \text{where } A = \max_{k \leq N} |a_k|.$$

Taking $\alpha < 1$ we have for each N that $z^{-N} R_N(z) \to 0$ uniformly in θ.

Lemma

$$|1 - e^{-z}| \leq |z| \quad \text{for Re } z \geq 0.$$

Proof

For $z = x$, a positive real number, it is a well-known elementary property which follows from the observation that the function $1 - x - \exp - x$ decreases monotonously. For complex z we write $z = x+iy$ and consider the function

$$f(x,y) = |1 - e^{-z}|^2 - |z|^2 = 1 - 2e^{-x}\cos y + e^{-2x} - x^2 - y^2.$$

Using the inequality $1 - \cos y \leq \tfrac{1}{2}y^2$, we have

$$f(x,y) = f(x,0) + 2e^{-x}(1-\cos y) - y^2 \leq$$

$$\leq f(x,0) + (e^{-x}-1)y^2 \leq f(x,0) \leq 0.$$

In some cases simpler methods are available for constructing an analytic function with a prescribed APS. Such a case arises when $\sum a_k z^k$ diverges for all z and $\sum a_k z^k/k!$ has a non-vanishing radius of convergence R. Then we may exploit the properties of the analytic function which for $|z| < R$ is defined by the latter series.

Example 3.3

Starting from the divergent power series $\sum_{k=0} (-1)^k k! z^k$, we consider the function $F(z) = \sum_{k=0} (-1)^k z^k = (1+z)^{-1}$. Formal integration of

$$f(z) = \int_0^\infty e^{-t} F(tz)dt,$$

i.e. by interchanging summation and integration, gives the original formal power series. Since $F(z)$ is holomorphic for all z with the exception of a pole at $z = -1$, the integral defines an analytic function which is holomorphic in the sector $-\pi < \arg z < \pi$, explicitly

$$f(z) = \int_0^\infty \frac{e^{-t}}{1+tz} dt.$$

According to example 2.1 this function has the required APS for real z. The next chapter will show that this result can be extended to complex z.

4. INTEGRATION BY PARTS

One of the simplest ways of finding the AE of a function defined by a definite integral is the method of integration by parts. However, the field of application is rather restricted. The method only works for definite integrals of a certain special kind. The idea will be made clear by treating a few particular examples.

As a first example we consider the error function

$$(4.1) \qquad \text{erf } x = \frac{2}{\sqrt{\pi}} \int_0^x e^{-t^2} dt.$$

We note that erf $(-x) = -$ erf x and erf $\infty = 1$. By expanding the integrand in its power series and integrating term by term, we obtain the series

$$(4.2) \qquad \tfrac{1}{2} \sqrt{\pi} \text{ erf } x = \sum_{k=0}^{\infty} \frac{(-1)^k}{2k+1} \frac{x^{2k+1}}{k!},$$

which is convergent for all values of x. However, for large values of $|x|$ the expansion ceases to be suitable for numerical calculation.
For large and positive values of x it is better to consider the complementary error function

$$(4.3) \qquad \text{erfc } x = \frac{2}{\sqrt{\pi}} \int_x^{\infty} e^{-t^2} dt.$$

The representation may be brought in the following form

$$\text{erfc } x = \pi^{-\frac{1}{2}} e^{-x^2} \int_0^{\infty} e^{-t} (t+x^2)^{-\frac{1}{2}} dt.$$

Applying integration by parts to the integral

$$f(x) = \int_0^{\infty} e^{-t} (t+x^2)^{-\frac{1}{2}} dt,$$

we find after one step

$$f(x) = x^{-1} - \tfrac{1}{2} \int_0^{\infty} e^{-t} (t+x^2)^{-3/2} dt,$$

and after n steps

$$(4.4) \qquad f(x) = \sum_{k=1}^{n} (-1)^{k-1} (\tfrac{1}{2})_{k-1} \, x^{-2k+1} + R_n(x),$$

where

$$(4.5) \qquad R_n(x) = (-1)^n (\tfrac{1}{2})_n \int_0^{\infty} e^{-t} (t+x^2)^{-n-\frac{1}{2}} dt.$$

The remainder has the sign of $(-1)^n$ and is in absolute value less than

$$(\tfrac{1}{2})_n \int_0^{\infty} e^{-t} x^{-2n-1} dt = (\tfrac{1}{2})_n k^{-2n-1}.$$

This result shows that the expansion (4.4) is an APS. It appears that in this particular case the AE has the pleasant property that the remainder after n terms is dominated by the (n+1)th term, i.e. the first omitted term. Thus we may write

$$(4.6) \qquad R_n(x) = \alpha(-1)^n (\tfrac{1}{2})_n x^{-2n-1}, \quad 0 < \alpha < 1.$$

The property (4.6) makes the expansion (4.4) extremely useful for numerical calculations although the formal power series

$$\sum_{k=0} (-1)^k (\tfrac{1}{2})_k x^{-2k-1}$$

diverges for all values of x.
Thus we have found the APS

$$(4.7) \qquad \operatorname{erfc} x \sim \pi^{-\frac{1}{2}} e^{-x^2} \sum_{k=0} (-1)^k (\tfrac{1}{2})_k x^{-2k-1}.$$

The analysis may easily be extended for complex values of x. However, the integral

$$f(z) = \int_0^{\infty} e^{-t} (t+z^2)^{-\frac{1}{2}} dt$$

can be used only for $|\arg z| < \tfrac{1}{2}\pi$. Repeating the analysis carried out above, we arrive at the same expression for the remainder (4.5). However, in view of the complex value of $t + z^2$ we have a different estimate

$$(4.8a) \qquad |R_n(z)| \leq (\tfrac{1}{2})_n \, |z|^{-2n-1}, \quad \text{for } |\arg z| \leq \tfrac{1}{4}\pi,$$

and

(4.8b) $|R_n(z)| \leq (\tfrac{1}{2})_n |z|^{-2n-1} |\sin 2\theta|^{-1}$, for $\tfrac{1}{4}\pi \leq |\arg z| < \tfrac{1}{2}\pi$.

The expansion is still suitable for the numerical calculation of erfc z provided z is not too close to the imaginary axis.
The estimate (4.8) shows that the expansion

(4.9) $\text{erfc } z \sim \pi^{-\frac{1}{2}} e^{-z^2} \sum_{k=0} (-1)^k (\tfrac{1}{2})_k z^{-2k-1}$

is an APS for $|\arg z| < \tfrac{1}{2}\pi$ and that it is a UAPS in any closed subsector.

Next we turn our attention to the function

(4.10) $f(z) = \int_0^\infty \frac{e^{-t}}{t+z} dt, \quad |\arg z| < \pi.$

This function is related to the incomplete gamma function

(4.11) $\Gamma(a,z) = \int_z^\infty e^{-t} t^{a-1} dt$

and we may write

(4.12) $f(z) = e^z \Gamma(0,z).$

It is not difficult to find the following series expansion

(4.13) $e^{-z} f(z) = -\log z - \gamma + \sum_{k=1}^\infty \frac{(-1)^{k-1} z^k}{k.k!},$

where $\gamma = -\int_0^\infty e^{-t} \log t \, dt$ is Euler's constant, which converges for all values of z. Again, the expansion ceases to be numerically useful for large values of $|z|$.
Integration of (4.10) by parts gives

$f(z) = z^{-1} - \int_0^\infty \frac{e^{-t}}{(t+z)^2} dt,$

and after n steps

$$(4.14) \qquad f(z) = \sum_{k=1}^{n} (-1)^{k-1}(k-1)! z^{-k} + R_n(z),$$

where

$$(4.15) \qquad R_n(z) = (-1)^n n! \int_0^\infty e^{-t}(t+z)^{-n-1} dt.$$

When z is real and positive the remainder has the sign of the first omitted term. A simple estimate shows that the remainder is also dominated by this term. For complex values of z we have

$$(4.16a) \qquad |R_n(z)| \leq n! \, |z|^{-n-1}, \text{ for } |\arg z| \leq \tfrac{1}{2}\pi,$$

and

$$(4.16b) \qquad |R_n(z)| \leq n! \, |z|^{-n-1} |\sin \theta|^{-n-1}, \text{ for } \tfrac{1}{2}\pi \leq |\arg z| < \pi.$$

These estimates show that

$$(4.17) \qquad \int_0^\infty \frac{e^{-t}}{t+z} \, dt \sim \sum_{k=0}^{} (-1)^k k! z^{-k-1}$$

is an APS for $|\arg z| < \pi$ and that it is a UAPS in any closed subsector.

The AE (4.17) can be used for the numerical calculation of $f(z)$, provided $|z|$ is not too small. If z is real and positive we write $z = x$ and $[x] = m$. The accuracy with which $f(x)$ can be obtained is determined by the behaviour of the remainder $R_n(x)$. However, since $R_n(x)$ is a rather complicated function of n we may as well take its estimate $n! x^{-n-1}$. The latter function is concave with a minimum for $n = m$. Thus the best result is obtained by stopping the expansion at the m-th term. The sign of the error is that of the first omitted term. The error is in absolute value less than $m! x^{-m-1}$, which may be replaced by the slightly rougher estimate $m! m^{-m-1}$. In the following table values of $^{10}\log (m^{m+1}/m!)$ are given which give an impression of the number of correct decimals which can be obtained by this method.

m	$^{10}\log (m^{m+1}/m!)$
2	0.6
3	1.1
4	1.6
5	2.1
6	2.6
7	3.1
8	3.5
9	4.0
10	4.4
11	4.9
12	5.3

5. BERNOULLI NUMBERS AND POLYNOMIALS

The Bernoulli numbers B_m, $m = 0,1,2,\ldots$ are defined by the expansion

(5.1) $\qquad \dfrac{t}{e^t - 1} = \sum\limits_{k=0}^{\infty} \dfrac{B_k}{k!}\, t^k, \quad |t| < 2\pi.$

All Bernoulli numbers with an odd index $m \geq 3$ are zero. This follows from the obvious fact that

$$\frac{t}{e^t - 1} + \tfrac{1}{2}t = \tfrac{1}{2}t \cot h \tfrac{1}{2}t$$

represents an even function of t.
The first few non-zero Bernoulli numbers are

$$
\begin{aligned}
&B_0 = 1 & &B_8 = -\frac{1}{30}\\
&B_1 = -\frac{1}{2} & &B_{10} = \frac{5}{66}\\
&B_2 = \frac{1}{6} & &B_{12} = -\frac{691}{2730}\\
&B_4 = -\frac{1}{30} & &B_{14} = \frac{7}{6}\\
&B_6 = \frac{1}{42} & &B_{16} = -\frac{3617}{510}\ .
\end{aligned}
$$

The Bernoulli polynomials $B_m(x)$, $m = 0,1,2,\ldots$ are defined by

(5.2) $\qquad \dfrac{te^{xt}}{e^t - 1} = \sum\limits_{k=0}^{\infty} \dfrac{B_k(x)}{k!}\, t^k, \quad |t| < 2\pi.$

The first few polynomials are

$$
\begin{aligned}
B_0(x) &= 1\\
B_1(x) &= x - \frac{1}{2}\\
B_2(x) &= x^2 - x + \frac{1}{6}\\
B_3(x) &= x^3 - \frac{3}{2}x^2 + \frac{1}{2}x\\
B_4(x) &= x^4 - 2x^3 + x^2 - \frac{1}{30}\\
B_5(x) &= x^5 - \frac{5}{2}x^4 + \frac{5}{3}x^3 - \frac{1}{6}x.
\end{aligned}
$$

The following relations are simple consequences of the definitions (5.1) and (5.2)

(5.3) $B_m(1-x) = (-1)^m B_m(x),$

(5.4) $B_m(0) = B_m,$

(5.5) $B_m'(x) = mB_{m-1}(x), \ m \geq 1.$

The Bernoulli numbers and the Bernoulli polynomials often appear in asymptotic expansions. We mention the following expansions

(5.6) $\log \Gamma(\omega+x) \sim (\omega+x-\tfrac{1}{2})\log \omega - \omega + \tfrac{1}{2} \log 2\pi +$

$$+ \sum_{k=1} (-1)^{k-1} \frac{B_{k+1}(x)}{k(k+1)} \omega^{-k}$$

valid for x constant and $\omega \to \infty,$

(5.7) $\log n! \sim (n+\tfrac{1}{2})\log n - n + \tfrac{1}{2} \log 2\pi +$

$$+ \sum_{k=1} \frac{B_{2k}}{2k(2k-1)} n^{-2k+1},$$

(5.8) $1 + \tfrac{1}{2} + \ldots + \dfrac{1}{n} - \log n \sim \gamma - \sum_{k=1} \dfrac{B_k}{k} n^{-k}.$

Proofs of these expansions are given later on in this section.

The asymptotic behaviour of the Bernoulli numbers can be derived from Cauchy's expression for the general coefficients of the power series expansion (5.1)

(5.9) $B_{2n}/(2n)! = \dfrac{1}{2\pi i} \oint \dfrac{dz}{z^{2n}(e^z-1)} , \ n \geq 1.$

The righthand side can be evaluated by taking the residues at $z = \pm 2k\pi i,$ $k = 1,2,3,\ldots$. This gives

(5.10) $B_{2n}/(2n)! = (-1)^{n-1} 2(2\pi)^{-2n} \displaystyle\sum_{k=1}^{\infty} \dfrac{1}{k^{2n}} ,$

which can be approximated by the asymptotic relation

(5.11) $B_{2n} \sim 2(-1)^{n-1} \dfrac{(2n)!}{(2\pi)^{2n}}$.

The Bernoulli polynomials $B_m(x)$ are closely related to the Euler functions $P_m(x)$ which are defined as periodic functions of period 1 and

(5.12) $P_m(x) = B_m(x)/m!$ for $0 \le x < 1$.

From the properties of the Bernoulli polynomials it follows that $P_m(x)$ is continuous except for m = 1. In particular

(5.13) $\begin{cases} P_0(x) = 1, \\[2mm] P_1(x) = x - [x] - \tfrac{1}{2}. \end{cases}$

Further we have

(5.14) $P'_{m+1}(x) = P_m(x)$,

and

(5.15) $P_m(b) \overset{\text{def}}{=} P_m(0) = B_m/m!$ for $m \ne 1$.

The saw tooth function $P_1(x)$ may be expanded in a Fourier series

(5.16) $P_1(x) = - \displaystyle\sum_{k=1}^{\infty} \dfrac{\sin 2k\pi x}{k\pi}$.

The higher Euler functions can be obtained from this by integration. In view of (5.15) we find

(5.17a) $P_{2m}(x) = 2(-1)^{m-1} \displaystyle\sum_{k=1}^{\infty} \dfrac{\cos 2k\pi x}{(2k\pi)^{2m}}$, $m \ge 1$,

(5.17b) $P_{2m+1}(x) = 2(-1)^{m-1} \displaystyle\sum_{k=1}^{\infty} \dfrac{\sin 2k\pi x}{(2k\pi)^{2m+1}}$, $m \ge 0$.

Again by using (5.15) we obtain the relation (5.10) by a different road.

The Euler functions appear in a well-known summation process usually named after Euler. In its simplest form we have the following formula

(5.18) $f(1) + f(2) + \ldots + f(n) = \int_1^n f(x)dx + \frac{1}{2}\{f(n) + f(1)\} +$

$$+ \int_1^n P_1(x)f'(x)dx,$$

where $f(x)$ has a continuous derivative for $x \geq 1$. The proof of (5.18) is almost trivial if one starts from the integral expression on the right-hand side

$$\int_0^n (x - [x] - \tfrac{1}{2})f'(x)dx.$$

Euler's summation formula (5.18) can be used for obtaining asymptotic expressions as will be shown in the following example.

Example 5.1

Taking $f(x) = x^{-1}$ we obtain from (5.18) the result

$$1 + \tfrac{1}{2} + \ldots + \frac{1}{n} = \log n + (\tfrac{1}{2} + \frac{1}{2n}) - \int_1^n x^{-2}P_1(x)dx.$$

For $n \to \infty$ we have

$$\gamma = \tfrac{1}{2} - \int_1^\infty x^{-2}P_1(x)dx$$

so that

$$1 + \tfrac{1}{2} + \ldots + \frac{1}{n} - \log n = \gamma + \frac{1}{2n} + \int_n^\infty x^{-2}P_1(x)dx.$$

This relation enables us to derive the asymptotic expansion (5.8) simply by partial integration of the integral on the right-hand side. Using the properties (5.14) and (5.15) we have

$$\int_n^\infty x^{-2}P_1(x)dx = - \frac{B_2}{2n^2} + 2 \int_n^\infty x^{-3}P_2(x)dx,$$

and after N-1 steps

$$\int_n^\infty x^{-2}P_1(x)dx = - \sum_{k=2}^N \frac{B_k}{k} n^{-k} + N! \int_n^\infty x^{-N-1}P_N(x)dx.$$

It is not difficult to show that the remainder is $O(n^{-N-1})$ by which the asymptotic behaviour is verified.

Example 5.2

Taking $f(x) = \log x$ we obtain from (5.18) the result

$$\log n! = (n+\tfrac{1}{2})\log n - n + 1 + \int_1^n x^{-1} P_1(x) dx.$$

For $n \to \infty$ we have according to Stirling's formula

$$\tfrac{1}{2} \log 2\pi = 1 + \int_1^\infty x^{-1} P_1(x) dx.$$

Combination of both results gives

$$\log n! = (n+\tfrac{1}{2})\log n - n + \tfrac{1}{2} \log 2\pi - \int_n^\infty x^{-1} P_1(x) dx.$$

In a similar way as in the preceding example by partial integration of the integral the asymptotic expansion (5.7) can be derived.

Example 5.3

Taking $f(x) = \log (x+a-1)$, $a > 0$ we obtain as in the more special case $a = 1$ discussed before

$$\log \Gamma(n+a) = (n+a-\tfrac{1}{2})\log n - n + \tfrac{1}{2} \log 2\pi - \int_n^\infty (x+a-1)^{-1} P_1(x) dx,$$

which can be developed into the asymptotic expansion (5.6).

6. LAPLACE INTEGRALS

We consider functions $f(z)$ of a complex variable z which are given by an integral of the form

$$(6.1) \qquad f(z) = \int_0^\infty e^{-zt} F(t)\,dt.$$

Such an integral is called a Laplace integral and $f(z)$ is called the Laplace tranform of $F(t)$. As a rule there exists a constant α such that the Laplace integral converges for Re $z > \alpha$ but diverges for Re $z < \alpha$. The constant α is called the abscissa of convergence and the region Re $z > \alpha$ the half-plane of convergence.

The function $f(z)$ is an analytic function holomorphic in the halfplane of convergence. It may happen that $\alpha = -\infty$. In that case $f(z)$ is an entire function.

Example 6.1

a. $F(t) = e^{-t}$ gives $f(z) = (z+1)^{-1}$ with $\alpha = -1$.

b. $F(t) = (1+t)^{-1}$ gives the special function (4.10) discussed in section 4. The Laplace representation (6.1) holds for Re $z > 0$ whereas the representation (4.10) holds in the wider region $|\arg z| < \pi$.

c. $F(t) = e^{-t^2}$ gives with $\alpha = -\infty$ the entire function

$$f(s) = \tfrac{1}{2}\sqrt{\pi}\, e^{z^2/4}\ \mathrm{erfc}\ \tfrac{1}{2}z.$$

d. $$F(t) = \begin{cases} (2t-t^2)^{-\frac{1}{2}} & \text{for } 0 \le t < 2 \\[2mm] 0 & \text{for } t \ge 2, \end{cases}$$

gives with $\alpha = -\infty$ the entire function

$$f(z) = \pi e^{-z} I_0(z).$$

For most applications it suffices to suppose that $F(t)$ is integrable and of exponential growth

$$(6.2) \qquad F(t) = O(e^{at}) \qquad \text{for } t \to \infty,$$

where a is a real constant.

Further we assume that for t → 0 there is an asymptotic expansion of the kind

(6.3) $F(t) \sim \sum_{k=0} a_k t^{\lambda_k}, \quad \lambda_0 > -1.$

However, in many applications for small values of t the integrand function is given by a convergent power series

(6.4) $F(t) = t^\mu \sum_{k=0}^{\infty} a_k t^k, \quad \mu > -1.$

In view of theorem 2.5 this expansion is also an APS of the kind (6.3).

Formally the AE of f(z) for z → ∞ is obtained from the AE (6.3) of F(t) by termwise integration. The resulting APS of f(z) holds for $|z| \to \infty$ and $|\arg z| < \frac{1}{2}\pi$ and is a UAPS in any smaller sector $|\arg z| \leq \frac{1}{2}\pi - \delta$. This important result rests upon a theorem known as Watson's lemma. However, before discussing this theorem we mention the following simple properties.

Theorem 6.1

(6.5) $\int_a^{\infty} e^{-zt} F(t)dt = O(e^{-a \, \mathrm{Re} \, z}),$

a > 0, for z → ∞ uniformly in $|\arg z| \leq \frac{1}{2}\pi - \delta$.

Proof

Without loss of generality we may assume that the integral exists for z = 0. Then we put $G(t) = \int_a^t F(t)dt$ so that G(t) is uniformly bounded, say by a constant M. Then we have

$$\left| \int_a^{\infty} a^{-zt} F(t)dt \right| = \left| z \int_a^{\infty} e^{-zt} G(t)dt \right| \leq M e^{-a \, \mathrm{Re} \, z} \, |z|/\mathrm{Re} \, z \leq$$

$$\leq M e^{-a \, \mathrm{Re} \, z}/\sin \delta.$$

For a = 0 the latter theorem may be improved somewhat. We have more generally

Theorem 6.2

(6.6) $\int_0^{\infty} e^{-zt} F(t)dt \to 0$ for $|z| \to \infty$ uniformly in $|\arg z| \leq \frac{1}{2}\pi - \delta$.

Proof

For any given ε > 0 we choose a such that

$$\left| \int_0^a e^{-zt} F(t) dt \right| \leq \int_0^a |F(t)| dt < \tfrac{1}{2} \varepsilon.$$

According to the preceding theorem there is a number ω such that

$$\left| \int_a^\infty e^{-zt} F(t) dt \right| < \tfrac{1}{2} \varepsilon \text{ for } |z| > \omega$$

uniformly in the sector $|\arg z| \leq \tfrac{1}{2}\pi - \delta$.
Thus for any ε there is a number ω(ε) such that

$$\left| \int_0^\infty e^{-zt} F(t) dt \right| < \varepsilon$$

for $|z| > \omega$ uniformly in the given sector.

Theorem 6.3 (Watson's lemma)

The asymptotic relation

(6.7) $F(t) = o(t^\mu)$ for $t \to 0$ with $\mu > -1$ implies

(6.8) $\displaystyle\int_0^\infty e^{-zt} F(t) dt = o(z^{-\mu-1})$, for $|z| \to \infty$ uniformly in the sector

$|\arg z| \leq \tfrac{1}{2}\pi - \delta$.

Proof

For any given ε > 0 there is a number a such that $|F(t)| \leq \tfrac{1}{2}\varepsilon t^\mu/\mu!$ for
t < a. Then we have

$$\left| \int_0^a e^{-zt} F(t) dt \right| \leq \tfrac{1}{2}\varepsilon \int_0^a e^{-xt} t^\mu/\mu! \ dt \leq \tfrac{1}{2}\varepsilon x^{-\mu-1}.$$

According to (6.5) there is a number ω such that

$$\left| \int_a^\infty e^{-zt} F(t) dt \right| \leq \tfrac{1}{2}\varepsilon x^{-\mu-1} \text{ for } x > \omega.$$

Thus for any ε there is a number ω(ε) such that

$$\left| \int_0^\infty e^{-zt} F(t) dt \right| \le \varepsilon x^{-\mu-1} \text{ for } x > \omega .$$

But this implies the statement (6.8).

Repeated use of Watson's lemma leads to the main theorem.

Theorem 6.4

The asymptotic power series

$$F(t) \sim \sum_{k=0}^\infty a_k t^{\lambda_k}, \; t \to 0,$$

implies the uniform asymptotic power series

(6.9) $$f(z) \sim \sum_{k=0}^\infty \lambda_k! a_k z^{-\lambda_k-1}, \; z \to \infty,$$

uniformly in any sector $|\arg z| \le \frac{1}{2}\pi - \delta$.

Example 6.2

According to example 6.1c we have

$$\int_0^\infty e^{-zt-\frac{1}{4}t^2} dt = \sqrt{\pi} e^{z^2} \text{erfc } z.$$

Formal integration of the series obtained by expanding the integrand function exp $-\frac{1}{4}t^2$ gives the APS (4.9) derived earlier by partial integration. However, no expression for a remainder term is obtained here.

Example 6.3

Taking $F(t) = (1+t)^{-1} = \sum_{k=0}^\infty t^k$ we obtain

$$\int_0^\infty e^{-zt}(1+t)^{-1} dt \sim \sum_{k=0}^\infty (-1)^t k! z^{-k-1},$$

an AE already discussed in section 4 (cf. formula (4.17)). However, the result is obtained here only for $|\arg z| < \frac{1}{2}\pi$ and again without explicit expression for the remainder.

Example 6.4

From example 6.1d we may derive an AE of the modified Bessel function

$I_0(z)$. Using the Laplace representation

$$\pi e^{-z} I_0(z) = 2^{-\frac{1}{2}} \int_0^2 e^{-zt} t^{-\frac{1}{2}} (1-\tfrac{1}{2}t)^{-\frac{1}{2}} dt,$$

we expand the integrand function as

$$2^{-\frac{1}{2}} t^{-\frac{1}{2}} (1-\tfrac{1}{2}t)^{-\frac{1}{2}} = \tfrac{1}{2} \sum_{k=0} \frac{(\tfrac{1}{2})_k}{k!} (\tfrac{1}{2}t)^{k-\frac{1}{2}}.$$

From (6.9) we obtain the AE

$$\pi e^{-z} I_0(z) \sim \sum_{k=0} \frac{(\tfrac{1}{2})_k (k-\tfrac{1}{2})!}{k!(2z)^{k+\frac{1}{2}}},$$

which will be written in the standard form

(6.10) $\qquad I_0(z) \sim \dfrac{e^z}{\sqrt{2\pi z}} \displaystyle\sum_{k=0} \dfrac{(\tfrac{1}{2})_k (\tfrac{1}{2})_k}{k!(2z)^k}$, $\quad |\arg z| < \tfrac{1}{2}\pi$.

As is shown in the examples given above, the asymptotic expansion of
(6.1) for $z \to \infty$ is obtained in the half-plane $|\arg z| < \tfrac{1}{2}\pi$. However, in
some cases the domain of validity can be extended to a wider sector. This
may happen by analytic continuation if the integrand function $F(t)$ is analytic, e.g. by rotation of the line of integration.

Example 6.5

Reconsidering example 6.3 we rotate the line of integration through an
angle $\tfrac{1}{2}\pi$. This gives

$$f(z) = \int_0^\infty e^{-izu} i(1+iu)^{-1} du$$

by which $f(z)$ is determined in the half-plane $-\pi < \arg z < 0$. The asymptotic
expansion (4.17) is now obtained for this sector. In a similar way by rotation through the angle $-\tfrac{1}{2}\pi$ the domain of validity is extended to the
sector $0 < \arg z < \pi$. Thus the AE (4.17) appears to hold in the full sector
$|\arg z| < \pi$ in accordance with the result obtained by integration by parts.
However, the latter method is still preferable.

The full power of the method of the Laplace integral is shown by its
application to the gamma function.

Starting from the well-known expansion

$$(6.11) \qquad \psi(z+1) = \frac{d}{dz} \log z! = -\gamma + \sum_{k=1}^{\infty} \left(\frac{1}{k} - \frac{1}{k+z}\right),$$

we may without difficulty verify that

$$(6.12) \qquad \psi(z+1) = -\gamma + \int_0^1 \frac{1-t^z}{1-t} \, dt, \quad \text{Re } z > -1.$$

This is equivalent with

$$\psi(z+1) = -\gamma - \log \varepsilon - \int_0^{1-\varepsilon} \frac{t^z}{1-t} \, dt + o(1) =$$

$$= -\gamma - \log \varepsilon - \int_{\varepsilon}^{\infty} \frac{e^{-zt}}{e^t-1} \, dt + o(1),$$

with $\varepsilon \to 0$.
On the other hand we have again for $\varepsilon \to 0$

$$-\gamma = \int_0^{\infty} e^{-t} \log t \, dt = \log \varepsilon + \int_{\varepsilon}^{\infty} e^{-t} t^{-1} dt + o(\varepsilon) =$$

$$= \log \varepsilon + \log z + \int_{\varepsilon}^{\infty} e^{-zt} t^{-1} dt + o(\varepsilon).$$

Combining these results we find the Laplace integral representation

$$(6.13) \qquad \psi(z+1) = \log z + \int_0^{\infty} e^{-zt} \left(\frac{1}{t} - \frac{1}{e^t-1}\right) dt, \quad \text{Re } z > 0.$$

The Laplace integral on the right-hand side of (6.13) can be expanded asymptotically by applying theorem 6.4. According to (5.1) we have

$$F(t) \sim - \sum_{k=0}^{\infty} \frac{B_{k+1}}{(k+1)!} t^k$$

so that

$$\psi(z+1) \sim \log z - \sum_{k=0} \frac{B_{k+1}}{k+1} z^{-k-1}$$

or

$$(6.14) \qquad \psi(z+1) \sim \log z + \frac{1}{2z} - \sum_{k=1} \frac{B_{2k}}{2k} z^{-2k}.$$

This AE is obtained at first for Re z > 0, but since it is possible to rotate the line of integration through angles $\pm \frac{1}{2}\pi$, the domain of validity of (6.14) can be extended to the sector $|\arg z| < \pi$.

The result (6.14) can be generalized without difficulty by starting from

$$(6.15) \qquad \psi(z+a) - \psi(z) = \int_0^\infty e^{-zt} \frac{e^t - e^{(1-a)t}}{e^t - 1} \, dt.$$

In view of (5.2), (5.3) and (5.4) we have for $|t| < 2\pi$

$$F(t) = \sum_{k=1}^\infty \frac{B_k(1) - B_k(1-a)}{k!} t^{k-1},$$

and next

$$(6.16) \qquad \psi(z+a) - \psi(z) \sim \sum_{k=1}^\infty (-1)^{k-1} \frac{B_k(a) - B_k}{k} z^{-k}.$$

Formal integration of (6.14) yields the AE of log z!. However, it is better to start from the integrated version of (6.13)

$$(6.17) \qquad \log z! = (z+\tfrac{1}{2})\log z - z + C + \int_0^\infty e^{-zt} \beta(t) dt,$$

where

$$(6.18) \qquad \beta(t) = \frac{1}{t} \left(\frac{1}{e^t - 1} - \frac{1}{t} + \frac{1}{2} \right) = \sum_{k=1}^\infty \frac{B_{2k}}{(2k)!} t^{2k-2}.$$

For Re z → ∞ the integral on the right-hand side of (6.17) is $O(z^{-1})$. Thus, in view of Stirling's formula, the constant of integration C equals $\frac{1}{2} \log 2\pi$. Formal substitution of the power series of $\beta(t)$, convergent only for $|t| < 2\pi$, gives the full AE already given by (5.7) for integer z.

$$(6.19) \qquad \log z! \sim (z+\tfrac{1}{2})\log z - z + \tfrac{1}{2} \log 2\pi + \sum_{k=1}^\infty \frac{B_{2k}}{2k(2k-1)} z^{-2k+1},$$

valid again for $|\arg z| < \pi$.

From (6.19) a generalization of the Stirling formula can be obtained by taking exponentials. We find

$$z! \sim z^{z+\frac{1}{2}} e^{-z} \sqrt{2\pi} \exp \left(\frac{1}{12z} - \frac{1}{360z^3} + \dots \right)$$

or

$$(6.20) \qquad z! \sim z^{z+\frac{1}{2}} e^{-z} \sqrt{2\pi} \; (1 + \frac{1}{12z} + \frac{1}{288z^2} + \dots).$$

The following example shows a related formula.

Example 6.6

For b > a we have

$$\frac{\Gamma(z+a)}{\Gamma(z+b)} = \frac{B(z+a,b-a)}{\Gamma(b-a)} = \frac{1}{\Gamma(b-a)} \int_0^1 t^{z+a-1} (1-t)^{b-a-1} dt.$$

In order to bring the integral into the form of a Laplace integral we perform the substitution t → exp-t. This gives

$$B(z+a,b-a) = \int_0^\infty e^{-zt} F(t) dt$$

with

$$F(t) = e^{-at} t^{b-a-1} \; (\frac{1-e^{-t}}{t})^{b-a-1}.$$

There remains as the only technical problem the expansion of F(t) into a power series. The first few terms are

$$F(t) = t^{b-a-1} - \frac{1}{2}(a+b-1)t^{b-a} + \dots .$$

From theorem 6.4 we then find the AE

$$(6.21) \qquad \frac{\Gamma(z+a)}{\Gamma(z+b)} \sim z^{-b+a} \{1 - \frac{1}{2}(b-a)(b+a-1)\frac{1}{z} + O(\frac{1}{z^2})\}.$$

This result derived only for b > a apparently also holds for a $\geq$ b.

7. FACTORIAL SERIES

We consider again the Laplace integral

$$(7.1) \qquad f(z) = \int_0^\infty e^{-zt} F(t) dt$$

but we make here the restriction that $F(t)$ is analytic and holomorphic in a domain which contains the positive real axis in its interior. This implies among others that for small values of $|t|$ the integrand function may be defined by its Taylor series

$$(7.2) \qquad F(t) = \sum_{k=0}^\infty a_k t^k.$$

We have seen in the previous section that substitution of (7.2) into (7.1) followed by formal integration yields an APS

$$(7.3) \qquad f(z) \sim \sum_{k=0}^\infty k! a_k z^{-k-1}.$$

However, in many cases the expansion (7.3) diverges and can be used for the numerical evaluation of $f(z)$ only for large values of $|z|$.
Better results may be obtained when $F(t)$ is expanded not as a Taylor series but with respect to a different set of functions $\{\psi_k\}$. In particular we shall consider the case $\psi_k = (1-e^{-t})^k$. The philosophy behind this choice is as follows. The asymptotic behaviour of $f(z)$ for $z \to \infty$ is determined by that of $F(t)$ for $t \to 0$. The power set $\{t^k\}$ and the set $\{\psi_k(t)\}$ are equivalent for $t \to 0$ so that it is plausible to expect that by using the latter set again an AE of $f(z)$ is obtained. However, the powers of $1 - e^{-t}$ are better adapted to the analytic properties of $F(t)$. This becomes apparent when one considers the conformal map

$$(7.4) \qquad u = 1 - e^{-t}.$$

The circle $|u| = 1$ is mapped upon the curve

$$(7.5) \qquad \text{Re } t = - \log (2 \cos \text{Im } t).$$

The illustration below shows that the region $|u| < 1$ corresponds to a region which contains the full positive real t-axis, a region of the kind where

F(t) is assumed to be holomorphic. Thus the latter method takes advantage from a larger region of holomorphy. Therefore better results may be expected.

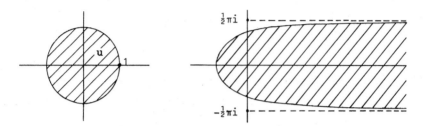

<u>fig. 7.1</u>

The formal procedure is as follows. Assuming the expansion

$$(7.6) \qquad F(t) = \sum_{k=0}^{\infty} b_k (1-e^{-t})^k,$$

we obtain the result

$$f(z) = \sum_{k=0}^{\infty} b_k \int_0^{\infty} e^{-zt}(1-e^{-t})^k dt.$$

Since

$$\int_0^{\infty} e^{-zt}(1-e^{-t})^t dt = \int_0^1 u^k(1-u)^{z-1} du = B(z,k+1) =$$

$$= \frac{k!}{z(z+1)\ldots(z+k)} ,$$

this result can be written as

$$(7.7) \qquad f(z) = \sum_{k=0}^{\infty} \frac{k!b_k}{z(z+1)\ldots(z+k)} .$$

This expansion is known as a factorial series. Series of the kind (7.7) are well-known in analysis. Their properties are studied extensively in Milne-Thomson. The series (7.7) is closely related to the Dirichlet series

$$(7.8) \qquad \sum_{k=0}^{\infty} b_k k^{-z} .$$

In fact they converge or diverge for the same values of z with the possible exception of the non-positive integers 0, -1, -2, ...
The proof of this property rests upon the simple asymptotic relation

$$(7.9) \qquad \frac{k}{(z+k)!} \sim k^{-z} \text{ for } k \to \infty,$$

which follows from (6.21) by specialization. Without proof we mention the following basic properties of a factorial series.

Theorem 7.1

If a factorial series converges for $z = z_0$, then it converges for Re $z >$ Re z_0 with the possible exception of non-positive integer values.

Theorem 7.2

If a factorial series converges for $z = z_0$, then it converges absolutely for Re $z > 1 +$ Re z_0 with the possible exception of non-positive integer values.

Theorem 7.3

If a factorial series converges absolutely for $z = z_0$, then it converges absolutely for Re $z >$ Re z_0 with the possible exception of non-positive integer values.

Theorem 7.4

If a factorial series converges for $z = z_0$, then it converges uniformly in any sector $|\arg(z-z_0)| \leq \frac{1}{2}\pi - \delta$ with the possible exclusion of small circular neighbourhoods at the points 0, -1, -2, ...

Theorem 7.5

The domain of convergence of a factorial series is a half-plane Re $z > \alpha$ with the exclusion of the points $z = 0, -1, -2, ...$.

In practical cases the abscissa of convergence α may easily be determined by using the asymptotic relation (7.9).

Example 7.1

The factorial series

$$\sum_{k=0}^{\infty} \frac{k!}{z(z+1)\ldots(z+k)}$$

converges for Re z > 1.

Example 7.2

We consider the Laplace integral

$$f(z) = \int_0^{\infty} e^{-zt}(e^t+1)^{-1}dt.$$

The integrand function is analytic and has simple poles on the imaginary axis $(2m+1)\pi i$, m integer. Thus the power series expansion

$$(e^t+1)^{-1} = \sum_{k=0}^{\infty} a_k t^k$$

converges only for $|t| < \pi$. From (5.1) we may obtain the explicit expression

$$a_k = -\frac{B_{k+1}}{(k+1)!}(2^{k+1}-1),$$

so that for k odd and large $|a_k| \sim 2\pi^{-k-1}$.
Substitution gives the APS

$$f(z) \sim \sum_{k=0}^{\infty} k! a_k z^{-k-1},$$

which, however, diverges for all values of z.
But, now performing the transformation (7.4), we have

$$f(z) = \int_0^1 (1-u)^z(2-u)^{-1}du.$$

The integrand function $(2-u)^{-1}$ can be expanded according to (7.6) into the power series

$$(2-u)^{-1} = \sum_{k=0}^{\infty} 2^{-k-1}u^k,$$

which is uniformly convergent for all values of u within the interval of integration. Interchanging the order of integration and summation is fully legitimate and we obtain the factorial series

$$f(z) = \sum_{k=0}^{\infty} \frac{2^{-k-1}k!}{(z+1)(z+2)\ldots(z+k+1)} \; .$$

This series converges for all values of z with the trivial exception z = -1, -2, ... Moreover, as will be shown below, it is an asymptotic expansion.

This example shows in an almost dramatic way how by a simple trick a divergent AE may be transformed into a convergent one. The transformation (7.4) applied to the Laplace integral replaces (7.1) by a representation of the kind

$$(7.10) \qquad f(z) = \int_0^1 (1-t)^{z-1} \phi(t) dt \; .$$

Formal expansion of $\phi(t)$ into a power series

$$(7.11) \qquad \phi(t) = \sum_{k=0}^{} b_k t^k$$

followed by formal integration gives the factorial series (7.7). If $\phi(t)$ is analytic and holomorphic in the circle $|t| < R$ with $R > 1$, the interchanging of integration and summation is permitted and the result is a factorial series which converges for all z with the exception of non-positive integers.
The asymptotic sequence $\phi_m(t) = t^m$, m = 0,1,2,... is transformed by (7.10) into the sequence

$$(7.12) \qquad \psi_m(z) = \frac{m!}{z(z+1)\ldots(z+m)} \; .$$

It is easy to convince oneself that the sequence (7.12) is an AS for $|z| \to \infty$ and that it can be used uniformly in any sector $|\arg z| \le \pi-\delta$. We may now state the analogon of Watson's lemma 6.3.

Theorem 7.6

The asymptotic relation

(7.13) $\phi(t) = o(t^m)$ for $t \to 0$

implies

(7.14) $\int_0^1 (1-t)^{z-1}\phi(t)dt = o(\psi_m)$ for $z \to \infty$

uniformly in any sector $|\arg z| \leq \frac{1}{2}\pi - \delta$.

Proof

Follows closely the proof of theorem 6.3 and may be left to the reader as
an exercise.

    This theorem like Watson's lemma guarantees the validity of the AE ob-
tained earlier by formal means.

In many cases, however, $\phi(t)$ is holomorphic in the unit circle or is at
least differentiable a number of times in the closed interval $(0,1)$. Then
a direct proof of the asymptotic property of the formal factorial series may
be obtained by integrating (7.10) by parts. After N steps we find

(7.15) $f(z) = \sum_{k=0}^{N} \frac{\phi^{(k)}(0)}{z(z+1)...(z+k)} + R_N(z),$

where

(7.16) $R_N(z) = \frac{1}{z(z+1)...(z+N)} \int_0^1 (1-t)^{z+N}\phi^{(N+1)}(t)dt.$

It is clear that the continuity of $\phi^{(N+1)}(t)$ implies the order relation
$R_N(z) = O(\psi_{N+1})$.

    Repeated use of theorem 7.6 gives the following analogon of theorem
6.4.

Theorem 7.7

The asymptotic power series

(7.17) $\phi(t) \sim \sum_{k=0}^{\infty} b_k t^k$, $t \to 0$

implies the uniform asymptotic factorial series

$$(7.18) \qquad f(z) \sim \sum_{k=0}^{\infty} \frac{k! b_k}{z(z+1)\ldots(z+k)}, \quad z \to \infty$$

uniformly in any sector $|\arg z| \leq \frac{1}{2}\pi - \delta$.

Example 7.3

In example 6.3 (cf. also formula (4.17)) we have found the APS

$$f(z) = \int_0^{\infty} e^{-zt}(1+t)^{-1}dt \sim \sum_{k=0}^{\infty} (-1)^k \, k! z^{-k-1}.$$

This expansion diverges for all values of z but can be used for numerical purposes if $|z|$ is sufficiently large. However, this expansion can be transformed into a factorial series which may be much better suited for numerical calculations. We write

$$f(z) = \int_0^1 (1-t)^{z-1} \phi(t) dt \text{ with}$$

$$\phi(t) = (1-\log(1-t))^{-1} = \sum_{k=0}^{\infty} b_k t^k.$$

It can be proved that $b_k = O(k^{-1} \log^{-2} k)$, $k \to \infty$. Therefore the power series converges uniformly in the interval of integration.
Hence the resulting factorial series (7.18) converges for Re $z > 0$.
The technical problem of determining the coefficients b_k can easily be solved by noting that

$$(1 + \sum_{k=1}^{\infty} t^k/k) \sum_{k=0}^{\infty} b_k t^k \equiv 1.$$

This gives the recurrent relation

$$b_k = - \sum_{j=0}^{k-1} \frac{b_j}{k-j}, \quad k \geq 1$$

with $b_0 = 1$.
The first few coefficients are

$$b_0 = 1, \quad b_1 = -1, \quad b_2 = \frac{1}{2}, \quad b_3 = -\frac{1}{3}.$$

Example 7.4

Starting from

$$\text{erfc }\sqrt{z} = \frac{1}{\sqrt{\pi}} \int_z^\infty e^{-t} t^{-\frac{1}{2}} dt$$

we obtain the Laplace integral representation

$$\text{erfc }\sqrt{z} = e^{-z} \sqrt{\frac{z}{\pi}} \int_0^\infty e^{-zt}(1+t)^{-\frac{1}{2}} dt.$$

Expansion of $(1+t)^{-\frac{1}{2}}$ into its Taylor series followed by formal integration would give the well-known AE obtained in example 6.1c and 6.2. This AE diverges for all values of z. But this representation may be transformed into

$$\pi^{\frac{1}{2}} z^{-\frac{1}{2}} e^{z} \text{ erfc }\sqrt{z} = \int_0^1 (1-t)^{z-1} \phi(t) dt,$$

with

$$\phi(t) = (1 - \log (1-t))^{-\frac{1}{2}}.$$

This function has a convergent Taylor series within the interval of integration as in the preceding example. Thus a convergent factorial series may be expected. We easily find

$$\phi(t) = 1 - \frac{1}{2} t + \frac{1}{8} t^2 - \frac{5}{48} t^3 + \dots ,$$

so that

(7.19) $$\text{erfc }\sqrt{z} \sim \frac{e^{-z}}{\sqrt{\pi z}} (1 - \frac{\frac{1}{2}}{z+1} + \frac{\frac{1}{4}}{(z+1)(z+2)} - \frac{\frac{5}{8}}{(z+1)(z+2)(z+3)} + \dots).$$

This AE, convergent for Re z > 0, may be compared to the divergent AE obtained in (4.9).

The analysis leading to a factorial series of the kind (7.7) can be generalized somewhat, eventually resulting in a factorial series of the form

(7.20) $$f(z) = \sum_{k=0}^{\infty} \frac{k! c_k(a)}{z(z+a)\dots(z+ka)} ,$$

where a is an arbitrary complex constant.

The general idea is that (7.20) always represents an asymptotic expansion for $|z| \to \infty$, but that for some values of a the series may converge and for other values of a may diverge. The effect of taking different values for a can be discussed by considering the representation (7.10). The convergence of the factorial series (7.7) resulting from the expansion (7.11) depends on the position of the singularities of $\phi(t)$. If there is at least one singularity inside the unit circle, the factorial series certainly diverges. However, if (7.10) is written as

$$(7.21) \qquad f(z) = \frac{1}{a} \int_0^1 (1-t)^{\frac{z}{a} - 1} \phi(1 - (1-t)^{1/a}) dt,$$

then formal expansion and integration of

$$(7.22) \qquad \phi(1 - (1-t)^{1/a}) = \sum_{k=0} c_k(a)(t/a)^k$$

results in the generalized factorial series (7.20). A singularity s of $\phi(t)$ corresponds to a singularity $1 - (1-s)^a$ of $\phi(1 - (1-t)^{1/a})$. This transformation

$$(7.23) \qquad s \to 1 - (1-s)^a$$

suggests that for suitable values of a the singularities of (7.22) are no longer inside the unit circle so that a convergent factorial series is obtained. If e.g. s is a negative real number with $-1 < s < 0$, then for a real and a $\log(1-s) > \log z$ the singularity is taken to the outside of the unit circle.

Complex values of a might be envisaged if (7.20) is used for the numerical computation of $f(z)$ for complex z. Then calculations may be facilitated by taking arg a = arg z.

Starting from the Laplace representation (7.1), the arbitrary constant may be introduced already at the beginning by writing (7.1) as

$$(7.24) \qquad f(z) = \frac{1}{a} \int_0^\infty e^{-tz/a} F(t/a) dt$$

and then performing the transformation (7.4).

Example 7.5

As in the preceding example we have

$$\pi^{\frac{1}{2}}z^{-\frac{1}{2}}e^{z} \text{ erfc } \sqrt{z} = \frac{1}{a}\int_{0}^{\infty} e^{-tz/a}(1 + t/a)^{-\frac{1}{2}}dt =$$

$$= \frac{1}{a}\int_{0}^{1} (1-t)^{z/a-1}\phi(t)dt \text{ with}$$

$$\phi(t) = (1 - a^{-1} \log(1-t))^{-\frac{1}{2}}.$$

The singularities are at $t = 1$ and $t = 1 - e^{a}$. Thus for $0 \le a < \log 2$ we obtain a divergent expansion and for $a > \log 2$ a convergent factorial series. The first few coefficients are

$$c_{0} = 1, \quad c_{1} = -\frac{1}{2}, \quad c_{2} = -\frac{1}{4} a + \frac{3}{8},$$

$$c_{3} = -\frac{1}{6} a^{2} + \frac{3}{8} a - \frac{5}{16}, \quad \ldots \quad .$$

We conclude this section by discussing another special case of the method sketched at the beginning. Starting again from the Laplace integral (7.1), we now expand the integrand function $F(t)$ in terms of $\psi_{k} = t^{k}(q+pt)^{-k-1}$, where p and q are positive real numbers with $p+q = 1$. The sets $\{t^{k}\}$ and $\{\psi_{k}(t)\}$ are asymptotically equivalent for $t \to 0$, therefore a new AE of $f(z)$ for $z \to \infty$ may be expected. Assuming as in (7.6) an expansion

$$(7.25) \qquad F(t) = \sum_{k=0}^{\infty} b_{k}t^{k}(q+pt)^{-k-1} \quad ,$$

we obtain the result

$$(7.26) \qquad qzf(z) = \sum_{k=0}^{\infty} b_{k}p^{-k}s_{k}(qz/p),$$

where the functions $s_{k}(\omega)$ are defined by

$$(7.27) \qquad s_{k}(\omega) = \omega\int_{0}^{\infty} e^{-\omega t}t^{k}(1+t)^{-k-1}dt.$$

This result is closely related to a transformation of a divergent or

slowly convergent series introduced by A. van Wijngaarden [21].
The functions $s_k(\omega)$ are studied from a numerical point of view by
N.M. Temme [18].
In fact, if to the series on the right-hand side of (7.3) the van Wijn-
gaarden transformation is applied the result (7.26) is obtained with
$p = q = \frac{1}{2}$.

The right-hand side of (7.26) is an AE with respect to the set
$\{s_k(\omega)\}$ with $\omega = qz/p$. Since asymptotically

$$(7.28) \qquad s_k(\omega) \sim k!\omega^{-k}, \quad -\pi < \arg \omega < \pi,$$

the sets $\{s_k(\omega)\}$ and $\{z^{-k}\}$ are asymptotically equivalent.
On the other hand the right-hand side of (7.26) may turn out to be convergent or perhaps rapidly convergent.
In section 9 (example 9.4) we derive the following asymptotic formula for
$s_k(\omega)$ as $k \to \infty$

$$(7.29) \qquad s_k(\omega) \sim \pi^{\frac{1}{2}} k^{-\frac{1}{4}} \omega^{\frac{3}{4}} \exp(\tfrac{1}{2}\omega - 2\sqrt{k\omega}).$$

The reason of this remarkable behaviour is the same as in the case of a
factorial series expansion. The powers of $t(p+qt)^{-1}$ are better adapted to
the analytic properties of $F(t)$ than the powers of t only.
Again we consider the corresponding conformal map

$$(7.30) \qquad u = \frac{t}{q+pt} \; .$$

Circular regions $|u| < c$ correspond to circular regions in the t-plane
bounded by Apollonius circles with respect to $t = 0$ and $t = -q/p$. In par-
ticular the circle $|u| < p^{-1}$ corresponds to the halfplane $\text{Re } t > -\tfrac{1}{2}q/p$.

Example 7.6

Again we take

$$(\pi z)^{\frac{1}{2}} e^z \text{ erfc } \sqrt{z} = z \int_0^\infty e^{-zt}(1+t)^{-\frac{1}{2}}dt.$$

The required expansion is

$$(1+t)^{-\frac{1}{2}} = \sum_{k=0}^{\infty} b_k t^k (q+pt)^{-k-1}$$

or

$$q(1-pu)^{-\frac{1}{2}} (1-pu+qu)^{-\frac{1}{2}} = \sum_{k=0}^{\infty} b_k u^k.$$

The radius of convergence is maximal for $p = 1/3$ and $q = 2/3$. This gives

$$\frac{2}{3} (1 - u^2/9)^{-1/2} = \sum_{k=0}^{\infty} b_k u^{2k}$$

with

$$b_k = \frac{2}{3} (\tfrac{1}{2})_k \frac{3^{-2k}}{k!} .$$

The final result is

$$(7.31) \qquad (\pi z)^{\frac{1}{2}} e^z \operatorname{erfc} \sqrt{z} = \sum_{k=0}^{\infty} \frac{(\tfrac{1}{2})_k}{k!} s_{2k}(2z).$$

The series is an AE and is moreover convergent for all z with $|\arg z| < \pi$.

8. THE EULER TRANSFORMATION

Generally speaking an asymptotic expansion of a given function $f(z)$ is not very suitable for the numerical calculation of $f(z)$. In some special cases only, the remainder of the finite expansion is kwnown to be comparable to the first neglected term. Sometimes the infinite expansion diverges for some or all values of z.

However, in many common applications the usefulness of an asymptotic series exceeds one's expectations. Moreover, the numerical analyst has at his disposal a number of tricks that may greatly improve his numerical results. The Euler transformation is perhaps the most used trick, at least it is most widely well-known. By means of this transformation it is sometimes possible to turn a divergent series into a convergent one.

Euler's transformation can be derived in the following elegant way. We consider a formal series

$$\sum a_k = a_0 + a_1 + a_2 + a_3 + \cdots$$

and introduce a formal shift operator S and the weighted mean operator M by means of

$$Sa_k = a_{k+1} \quad ,$$

$$M = p + qS \qquad \text{with } |p| < 1 \text{ and } q = 1 - p.$$

Then we have formally

$$\sum a_k = \sum S^k a_0 = \frac{a_0}{1-S} = \frac{qa_0}{1-M} = q\sum M^k a_0.$$

This formal procedure suggests the Euler transformation of type $E(q)$

$$b_k = qM^k a_0$$

or explicitly

$$(8.1) \qquad b_k = \sum_{j=0}^{k} \binom{k}{j} p^{k-j} q^{j+1} a_j.$$

The numerical analyst who does not care for theory asserts that $\sum b_k$ is a better series than $\sum a_k$. Usually the process is carried out with $p = q = \frac{1}{2}$ and if necessary carried out a number of times until a good series is obtained.

If, by way of illustration, the following alternating series

$$1 - \frac{1}{2} + \frac{1}{3} - \frac{1}{4} + \ldots$$

is "eulerized", we obtain

$$\frac{1}{1.2} + \frac{1}{2.2^2} + \frac{1}{3.2^3} + \frac{1}{4.2^4} + \ldots \quad ,$$

the convergence of which is much better than that of the original series.

In order to get a better insight into the effect of an Euler transformation we consider the generating functions

$$(8.2) \qquad a(z) = \sum a_k z^{k+1} \; , \; b(z) = \sum b_k z^{k+1} \; .$$

We restrict our discussion preliminary to those series for which $a(z)$ has a non-vanishing radius of convergence R_a. This enables us to handle divergent series such as $1 - 2 + 3 - 4 + \ldots$ but a series like $1! - 2! + 3! - 4! + \ldots$ falls outside this class.

It is easily seen by comparing equal powers of z that the relation (8.1) is equivalent with

$$(8.3) \qquad b(z) = a(\frac{qz}{1-pz}) \; .$$

The radius of convergence of $a(w)$, where

$$(8.4) \qquad w = \frac{qz}{1-pz} \quad , \quad z = \frac{w}{q+pw} \; ,$$

is determined by the singularities $w = s$ of the holomorphic function $a(w)$ as

$$(8.5) \qquad R_a = \inf |s| \; .$$

Then the radius of convergence of $b(z)$ is given by

(8.6) $R_b = \inf \left| \dfrac{s}{q+ps} \right|$.

The Euler method is most effective if R_b/R_a is as large as possible.

Example 8.1.

For the example given above we have the generating function $a(z) = \log(1+z)$. According to (8.3) we have $b(z) = - \log(1-\frac{1}{2}z)$ with a radius of convergence which is twice as large. More generally, if $a(z)$ has its singularities at $z = -1$ and $z = \infty$, then $b(z)$ is singular for $z = (p-q)^{-1}$ and $z = p^{-1}$. The ordinary Euler transformation $E(\frac{1}{2})$ gives $R_a = 1$ and $R_b = 2$. However, the transformation with $p = 1/3$, $q = 2/3$ gives even better $R_b = 3$.

In an alternative way the Euler method may be discussed by considering the generating functions

(8.7) $\alpha(z) = \sum_k a_k z^k/k!$, $\beta(z) = \sum_k b_k z^k/k!$.

The relation (8.1) is easily seen to be equivalent with the functional equation

(8.8) $e^{-z}\beta(z) = qe^{-qz}\alpha(qz)$.

It clearly suffices to consider the coefficient of z^k in the expansion of $q\alpha(qz)\exp pz$.

From (8.8) we obtain the interesting result that the operators $E(q)$ form a commutative semigroup with the property

(8.9) $E(q_1)E(q_2) = E(q_1q_2)$.

We shall now extend the discussion of the Euler method to those series $\sum a_k$ for which $\alpha(z)$ is holomorphic in a domain which contains the positive real axis. If

(8.10) $A = \displaystyle\int_0^\infty e^{-x}\alpha(x)dx$

exists, the series is said to be <u>Borel summable</u> with A as its <u>Borel sum</u>.

From (8.7) and (8.8) it follows at once

Theorem 8.1

The Euler transformation E(q) with q real and positive does not change
the Borel sum.

Proof

$$\int_0^\infty e^{-x} \beta(x) dx = q \int_0^\infty e^{-qx} \alpha(qx) dx = \int_0^\infty e^{-x} \alpha(x) dx.$$

A summation method such as the Euler transformation which turns a convergent series into a convergent series with the same sum is said to be
regular. For summation methods of the type (8.10) regularity is defined in
the same way. The following property is proved in Hardy [6,8.5] in a
more general context.

Theorem 8.2

The Borel method (8.10) is regular.

Proof

We put for k = 0,1,2,...

$$\phi_k(x) = \frac{1}{k!} \int_x^\infty e^{-t} t^k dt = e^{-x}(1+x+\frac{x^2}{2!}+\ldots+\frac{x^k}{k!})$$

and

$$\psi_k(x) = e^{-x} x^k / k! \ .$$

If
$$\sum a_k = A \text{ and } \sum_{j=k}^\infty a_k = A_k, \text{ then}$$

$$\int_0^x e^{-t} \alpha(t) dt = \sum \frac{a_k}{k!} \int_0^x e^{-t} t^k dt = \sum a_k(1-\phi_k) =$$

$$= A - \sum a_k \phi_k = A - \sum (A_k - A_{k+1})\phi_k =$$

$$= A - \sum A_k \psi_k .$$

Hence there remains to prove that

$$\lim_{x\to\infty} e^{-x}\sum_k A_k x^k/k! = 0,$$

but this is an elementary matter.

Hardy gives necessary and sufficient conditions for the regularity of a wide class of summation methods. The regularity of the Euler transformation appears to be a simple corollary.

It has been seen in the preceding chapter that many asymptotic expansions originate from Laplace integrals. Summation of the asymptotic series means in fact the evaluation of the Laplace integral for a particular value of the Laplace variable. Taking the expression (8.10) as a typical case, one is inclined to reason as follows. In view of the formal relation

$$(8.11) \qquad \int_0^\infty e^{-x}\alpha(x)dx = \sum a_k,$$

the integral can be evaluated by summing the series either directly or after one or more Euler transformations. However, the proof of theorem 8.1 clearly shows that one may save oneself the trouble of "eulerizing", since the same effect may be obtained in a much simpler way by performing an almost trivial transformation of the integrand. We write

$$(8.12) \qquad \int_0^\infty e^{-x}\alpha(x)dx = \int_0^\infty e^{-\mu x}\{e^{-(1-\mu)x}\alpha(x)\}dx$$

and subject the new integrand function to a power series expansion

$$(8.13) \qquad \mu^{-1}e^{-(1-\mu)x}\alpha(x) = \sum \frac{b_k}{k!}(\mu x)^k.$$

The result of formally integrating the new series is the Euler transformation with $q = \mu^{-1}$.

Example 8.1

According to example 6.3 we have the AE

$$\int_0^\infty e^{-xt}(1+t)^{-1}dt \sim \sum_{k=0} (-1)^k k!x^{-k-1}, \qquad\qquad x \to +\infty.$$

The AE diverges for all values of x but we have seen already in section 4
that for large values of x accurate numerical results can be obtained by
truncation at the right place. For x = 1 the series

$$1 - 1! + 2! - 3! + 4! - 5! + \ldots$$

seems to offer no hope. Yet the ordinary Euler process gives a "less divergent" result

$$\frac{1}{2} + 0 + \frac{1}{8} - \frac{1}{8} + \frac{9}{32} - \frac{11}{16} + \frac{265}{128} - \ldots .$$

Repeated application of the Euler transformation eventually leads to a
usable series yielding the numerical value 0.596347.

The Euler transformation may be circumvented by writing

$$\int_0^\infty e^{-t}(1+t)^{-1} dt = \int_0^\infty e^{-x} \frac{qe^{px}}{1+qx} dx$$

and applying power series expansion of the new integrand function. Instead
of repeating the Euler transformation if the resulting series is not good
enough, we merely have to choose a proper value of q. It can be expected
that smaller values of q give better results but that it takes more trouble
to get a final result.

9. THE METHOD OF LAPLACE

In this section we consider the asymptotic behaviour of functions $f(\omega)$ of the type

$$(9.1) \qquad f(\omega) = \int_{-\infty}^{\infty} F(t,\omega)\,dt,$$

where the integrand function has the shape of a hill tending to a peak or a needle as $\omega \to +\infty$. The basic idea can be illustrated by considering the asymptotic behaviour of the factorial function

$$(9.2) \qquad \omega! = \int_{0}^{\infty} e^{-t} t^{\omega} dt.$$

The integrand is a hill with its summit at $t = \omega$. It may be a good idea to shift this summit to the origin by performing the substitution $t = \omega(1+u)$. This gives

$$(9.3) \qquad \omega! = e^{-\omega} \omega^{\omega+1} \int_{-1}^{\infty} \{e^{-u}(1+u)\}^{\omega} du.$$

The new integrand represents again a hill but its summit is fixed at the origin. For large values of ω the hill becomes a needle. In fact, near the origin we may write

$$(9.4) \qquad e^{-u}(1+u) = \exp\{-u + \ln(1+u)\} = \exp(-\tfrac{1}{2}u^2 + \ldots).$$

Thus we have approximately

$$(9.5) \qquad \omega! \sim e^{-\omega} \omega^{\omega+1} \int_{-1}^{\infty} e^{-\frac{1}{2}u^2 \omega} du$$

and with an almost equal precision

$$(9.6) \qquad \omega! \sim e^{-\omega} \omega^{\omega+1} \int_{-\infty}^{\infty} e^{-\frac{1}{2}u^2 \omega} du.$$

Working out the integration we obtain Stirling's well-known approximation

$$(9.7) \qquad \omega! \sim e^{-\omega} \omega^{\omega} \sqrt{2\pi\omega}.$$

It is not difficult to make this analysis completely rigorous. We shall therefore consider more generally the asymptotic behaviour of the integral

(9.8) $$f(\omega) = \int_{-\infty}^{\infty} e^{-\omega\phi(t)} dt$$

for real ω tending to infinity. Then we may state the following theorem.

Theorem 9.1

Let $\phi(t)$ be a concave function with its minimum at $t = t_0$, let $\phi(t)$ be continuously differentiable in a neighbourhood of t_0 with

(9.9) $$\phi(t) = \phi(t_0) + \tfrac{1}{2}a(t-t_0)^2 + O((t-t_0)^3) ,$$

then we have the following asymptotic relation

(9.10) $$\int_{-\infty}^{\infty} e^{-\omega\phi(t)} dt = (\frac{2\pi}{a\omega})^{\frac{1}{2}} e^{-\omega\phi(t_0)} (1+O(\omega^{-\frac{1}{2}})).$$

Proof

Without loss of generality we may take $t_0 = 0$ and $\phi(t_0) = 0$. There exist positive constants c and δ such that

$$|\phi(t)-\tfrac{1}{2}at^2| < c|t|^3 \text{ for } |t| < \delta.$$

Then in view of theorem 6.1 we may write

$$\int_{-\infty}^{\infty} e^{-\omega\phi(t)} dt = \int_{-\delta}^{\delta} e^{-\omega\phi(t)} dt + O(\omega^{-\infty}) =$$

$$= \int_{-\delta}^{\delta} e^{-\frac{1}{2}a\omega t^2} dt + \int_{-\delta}^{\delta} e^{-\frac{1}{2}a\omega t^2} \{e^{-\omega(\phi(t)-\frac{1}{2}at^2)}-1\} dt + O(\omega^{-\infty}).$$

The first term is

$$\int_{-\infty}^{\infty} e^{-\frac{1}{2}a\omega t^2} dt + O(\omega^{-\infty}) = (\frac{2\pi}{a\omega})^{\frac{1}{2}} + O(\omega^{-\infty}).$$

With the help of the inequality

$$|e^t-1| < |t|e^{|t|}$$

the second term can be majorized by

$$2c\omega \int_0^\delta \exp - (\tfrac{1}{2}a\omega t^2 - c\omega t^3)t^3 dt \leq$$

$$2c\omega \int_0^\delta \exp(-(\tfrac{1}{2}a - \delta c)\omega t^2)t^3 dt \leq$$

$$2c\omega \int_0^\infty e^{-b\omega t^2}t^3 dt = 0(\omega^{-1}),$$

where for sufficiently small δ

$$b = \tfrac{1}{2}a - \delta c > 0.$$

Combining these results we obtain the relation (9.10).

It will be obvious that the conditions of this theorem may be varied in a number of ways. The only thing that matters is that $\phi(t)$ has an absolute minimum at t_0 and that in a neighbourhood of t_0 this function is sufficiently smooth. If $\phi(t) \geq \phi(t_0) + \varepsilon$ for $|t-t_0| \geq \delta$ with some positive ε, we need only consider the δ-neighbourhood of t_0. If $\phi(t)$ is differentiable a number of times, we have $a = \phi(t_0)$. Further, the relative remainder may admit a better estimate than the term with $\omega^{-\frac{1}{2}}$.

Example 9.1

If $\qquad \phi(t) = t^2(1+|t|)$, $\qquad\qquad$ we have

$$f(\omega) = (\frac{\pi}{\omega})^{\frac{1}{2}} - \frac{1}{\omega} + \ldots .$$

Example 9.2

If $\qquad \phi(t) = t^2 \sqrt{1+t^2}$, $\qquad\qquad$ we have

$$f(\omega) = (\frac{\pi}{\omega})^{\frac{1}{2}} (1 - \frac{3}{8\omega} + \ldots) .$$

Example 9.3

For the integral

$$\int_0^1 t^{\alpha\omega}(1-t)^{\beta\omega}dt \qquad\qquad \text{with } \alpha > 0,\ \beta > 0$$

we have

$$\phi(t) = -\alpha \log t - \beta \log(1-t),$$

which is concave with $t_0 = \alpha(\alpha+\beta)^{-1}$,
and further

$$a = \phi''(t_0) = \frac{\alpha}{t_0^2} + \frac{\beta}{(1-t_0)^2} = \frac{(\alpha+\beta)^3}{\alpha\beta}.$$

The relation (9.10) gives at once the asymptotic behaviour

$$(2\pi\alpha\beta)^{\frac{1}{2}}\ (\alpha+\beta)^{-3/2}\ \frac{\alpha^{\alpha\omega}\beta^{\beta\omega}}{\omega^{\frac{1}{2}}(\alpha+\beta)^{(\alpha+\beta)\omega}}.$$

Of course the given integral may easily be expressed in gamma functions so that the result obtained above can also be derived by using the Stirling approximation. However, use of (9.10) is simpler.

Example 9.4

The derivation of the asymptotic expression (7.29) from (7.27) illustrates the treatment of a more complicated case. We start from

$$f(k) = \int_0^\infty e^{-\phi(t)}dt,$$

where

$$\phi(t) = (k+1) \log (t+1) - k \log t + \omega t$$

so that in the notation of (7.27) $f(t) = s_k(\omega)/\omega$.
We note that here ω is a parameter and that k is the asymptotic variable. The integrand has its maximum at $t = t_0$ where t_0 is the positive root of

$$\phi'(t) = \omega - \frac{k}{t} + \frac{k+1}{t+1} = 0.$$

We have

$$t_0 = \sqrt{\frac{k}{\omega}} - \frac{\omega+1}{2\omega} + \cdots .$$

Then we have

$$f(k) \sim e^{-\phi(t_0)} \int_{-\infty}^{\infty} e^{-\frac{1}{2}\phi''(t_0)(t-t_0)^2} dt .$$

A simple calculation gives

$$\phi(t_0) = 2\sqrt{k\omega} + \frac{1}{2} \log \frac{k}{\omega} - \frac{1}{2}\omega + O(k^{-\frac{1}{2}}) ,$$

and

$$\phi''(t_0) = 2k^{-\frac{1}{2}}\omega^{3/2} + O(k^{-1}) .$$

With the omission of the order terms we then obtain

$$f(k) \sim (\pi k^{\frac{1}{2}}\omega^{-3/2})^{\frac{1}{2}} \exp -(2\sqrt{k\omega}+\frac{1}{2}\log\frac{k}{\omega}-\frac{1}{2}\omega).$$

From this (7.29) follows at once.

For the slightly more general integral representation

(9.11) $$f(\omega) = \int_{-\infty}^{\infty} e^{-\omega\phi(t)}\psi(t)dt$$

similar results may be obtained. If $\phi(t)$ has the properties stated in
theorem 9.1 and if $\psi(t)$ is, say, continuously differentiable in a neighbourhood of t_0, the result (9.10) may be generalized as

(9.12) $$\int_{-\infty}^{\infty} e^{-\omega\phi(t)}\psi(t)dt = (\frac{2\pi}{a\omega})^{\frac{1}{2}} e^{-\omega\phi(t_0)} \psi(t_0)(1+O(\omega^{-\frac{1}{2}})) .$$

In some cases the following method may be recommanded. A new variable
u is introduced by means of

(9.13) $\qquad au^2 = \phi(t) - \phi(t_0)$

where u has the sign of $t - t_0$. The transformation $t \rightarrow u$ is monotonous in some neighbourhood of t_0. Since this neighbourhood is decisive for the asymptotic behaviour of $f(\omega)$, we do not care what happens elsewhere. Formal substitution of (9.13) in (9.11) gives the asymptotic relation

(9.14) $\qquad f(\omega) \sim e^{-\omega\phi(t_0)} \int_{-\infty}^{\infty} e^{-a\omega u^2} \chi(u)du,$

$$\chi(u) = \psi(t)dt/du \ .$$

The last integral may be considered as a variant of the Laplace integral to which it can be reduced by changing the variable of integration u into $\pm u^{\frac{1}{2}}$. According to theorem 6.4 there remains to determine the power series expansion of $\chi(u)$ in powers of u.

10. CALCULATION OF COEFFICIENTS

We consider the asymptotic expansion of the integral

$$(10.1) \qquad f(\omega) = \int_{-\infty}^{\infty} e^{-\omega\phi(t)} \psi(t)dt.$$

We assume that $\phi(t)$ is concave with a zero minimum at $t = 0$. Further it is assumed that $\phi(t)$ and $\psi(t)$ admit Taylor expansions convergent in a neighbourhood of $t = 0$.

Starting with the simple but representative case

$$(10.2) \qquad \phi(t) = \tfrac{1}{2}t^2$$

and the Taylor expansion

$$(10.3) \qquad \psi(t) = \sum_{k=0}^{\infty} b_k t^k$$

the asymptotic expansion of (10.1) can be written down at once as

$$f(\omega) \sim \sum_{k=0}^{\infty} b_k \int_{-\infty}^{\infty} e^{-\frac{1}{2}\omega t^2} t^k dt,$$

or

$$(10.4) \qquad f(\omega) \sim (\tfrac{2\pi}{\omega})^{\frac{1}{2}} \sum_{k=0}^{\infty} 1.3.5 \cdots (2k-1) b_{2k} \omega^{-k}.$$

We note that the coefficients of $\psi(t)$ with an odd index do not contribute to the expansion.

If, more generally, $\phi(t)$ is determined by the following Taylor series

$$(10.5) \qquad \phi(t) = \sum_{k=2}^{\infty} a_k t^k \,, \quad a_2 > 0,$$

we may perform the substitution

$$(10.6) \qquad \tfrac{1}{2}u^2 = \phi(t)$$

which for small t and u is equivalent to

$$(10.7) \qquad u = t\sqrt{2a_2} + 0(t^2).$$

58

We obtain

$$(10.8) \qquad f(\omega) \sim \int_{-\infty}^{\infty} e^{-\frac{1}{2}\omega u^2} \psi(t) \frac{dt}{du} du \ ,$$

so that in view of (10.1), (10.3) and (10.4) there remains to determine the coefficients of the Taylor expansion of $\psi(t) dt/du$

$$(10.9) \qquad \psi(t) \frac{dt}{du} = \sum_{k=0}^{\infty} c_k u^k \ .$$

Example 10.1

We consider

$$f(\omega) = \int_{-1}^{\infty} \exp - \omega(t - \log(1+t)) dt \ .$$

According to (9.3) we have

$$f(\omega) = e^{\omega} \omega^{-\omega-1} \omega! \ .$$

The Taylor series (10.5) is

$$\phi(t) = \frac{1}{2} t^2 - \frac{1}{3} t^3 + \frac{1}{4} t^4 - \dots \ .$$

The substitution (10.6) becomes

$$u = t - \frac{1}{3} t^2 + \frac{7}{36} t^3 - \dots \ .$$

We need, however, the inverse expansion

$$t = u + \frac{1}{3} u^2 + \frac{1}{36} u^3 + \dots \ .$$

Differentiation gives

$$c_0 = 1 \ , \quad c_1 = \frac{2}{3} \ , \quad c_2 = \frac{1}{12} \ , \quad \dots \ .$$

This gives us already two terms of the asymptotic expansion of $f(\omega)$

$$\frac{\omega!}{\omega^{\omega+\frac{1}{2}} e^{-\omega} \sqrt{2\pi}} \sim 1 + \frac{1}{12\omega} + \dots \ .$$

It seems that the calculation of further coefficients becomes increasingly complicated. However, by differentiation of

$$\tfrac{1}{2}u^2 = t - \log(1+t),$$

we obtain

$$u\frac{du}{dt} = \frac{t}{1+t}$$

or

$$t\frac{dt}{du} = (1+t)u.$$

Substitution of

$$t = \sum_{k=1}^{\infty} d_k u^k$$

leads to the recurrence relation

$$\sum_{j=1}^{k} jd_j d_{k-j+1} = d_{k-1} \quad , \qquad k \gtrless 2$$

together with $d_1 = 1$.
This gives $d_2 = \frac{1}{3}$ and

$$(k+1)d_k = d_{k-1} - \sum_{j=2}^{k-1} jd_j d_{k-j+1} \quad , \qquad k \geq 3,$$

so that successive coefficients can be calculated in a simple way. We find

$$d_1 = 1 \quad , \quad d_2 = \frac{1}{3} \quad , \quad d_3 = \frac{1}{36} ,$$

$$d_4 = -\frac{1}{270} \quad , \quad d_5 = \frac{1}{4320} \quad \text{etc. .}$$

Since $c_k = (k+1)d_{k+1}$, we obtain a further term in the asymptotic expansion of $f(\omega)$ as

(10.10) $\qquad \dfrac{\omega!}{\omega^{\omega+\frac{1}{2}}e^{-\omega}\sqrt{2\pi}} \sim 1 + \dfrac{1}{12\omega} + \dfrac{1}{288\omega^2} + O(\omega^{-3})$.

The coefficients c_k of the Taylor expansion (10.9) can also be derived by using the well-known Lagrange-Bürmann theorem which gives formulae for the coefficients of the expansion of a function in powers of some other function. The same result may be obtained with the help of the Cauchy formula for the coefficient of the Taylor expansion of an analytic function. Starting from

$$c_k = \frac{1}{2\pi i} \oint \frac{\psi(w)dw/dz}{z^{k+1}} \, dz$$

with the complex version of (10.6)

$$z = \sqrt{2\phi(w)} \, ,$$

we have

$$c_k = \frac{1}{2\pi i} \oint \frac{\psi(w)(w/z)^{k+1}}{w^{k+1}} \, dw \ .$$

This means that c_k equals the coefficient of w^k in the expansion of

$$\psi(w) \left(\frac{w}{\sqrt{2\phi(w)}} \right)^{k+1}$$

in powers of w.

We next present a quite different method which in some cases may be very successful.

We write formally

(10.11) $\qquad \psi(t)e^{-\omega\phi(t)} = e^{-\frac{1}{2}u^2} \displaystyle\sum_{k=0}^{\infty} P_k(u)\omega^{-k/2}$,

where $u = t\omega^{\frac{1}{2}}$. Substitution in (10.1) gives at once the AE

(10.12) $\qquad f(\omega) \sim \displaystyle\sum_{k=0}^{\infty} \omega^{-\frac{k+1}{2}} \int_{-\infty}^{\infty} e^{-\frac{1}{2}u^2} P_k(u)du$.

Example 10.2

Taking the same integral as in the first example we have

$$\sum_{k=0}^{\infty} p_k(u)\omega^{-k/2} = \exp - \omega(\phi-\tfrac{1}{2}t^2) =$$

$$= \exp \omega(\tfrac{1}{2}t^3-\tfrac{1}{4}t^4+\ldots) =$$

$$= \exp(\tfrac{1}{3}u^3\omega^{-\frac{1}{2}}-\tfrac{1}{4}u^4\omega^{-1}+\ldots) \ .$$

This shows that the coefficients $p_k(u)$ are polynomials of degree 3k.
The first few coefficients are

$$p_0 = 1 \qquad\qquad p_3 = \tfrac{1}{5}u^5 - \tfrac{1}{12}u^7 + \tfrac{1}{162}u^9$$

$$p_1 = \tfrac{1}{3}u^3 \qquad\qquad p_4 = -\tfrac{1}{6}u^6 + \tfrac{47}{480}u^8 - \tfrac{1}{72}u^{10} + \tfrac{1}{1944}u^{12} \ .$$

$$p_2 = -\tfrac{1}{4}u^4 + \tfrac{1}{18}u^6$$

Substitution in (10.12) eventually leads to the result (10.10).

The polynomials may be calculated by a recurrence relation which is obtained as follows.
If we write

$$F(u) = \sum_{k=0}^{\infty} p_k(u)\omega^{-k/2} ,$$

we find by logarithmic differentiation of

$$F(u) = \exp(-\omega\phi+\tfrac{1}{2}u^2)$$

the differential equation

$$(u+\omega^{\frac{1}{2}})F' = u^2 F.$$

Substitution of the power series on both sides leads to the relation

$$up_k' + p_{k+1}' = u^2 p_k, \qquad\qquad k \geq 1.$$

In view of the obvious fact that $p_k(0) = 0$ for $k \geq 1$, we find by integration the recurrence relation

$$p_{k+1}(u) = up_k(u) + \int_0^u (1+\eta^2)p_k(\eta)d\eta, \qquad\qquad k \geq 1.$$

The methods explained above for finding the coefficients of an APS are very effective. Still in special cases a more powerful method with less amount of labour may be available.

For instance, the AE of $\omega!$ can be obtained from the well-known AE of log $\omega!$ simply by exponentiation according to

$$(10.13) \qquad \sum_{k=0}^{\infty} a_k x^k = \exp \sum_{k=1}^{\infty} b_k x^k \,,$$

where the coefficients b_k are known. Formal differentiation gives

$$\sum_{k=1}^{\infty} k a_k x^{k-1} = \sum_{k=0}^{\infty} a_k x^k \cdot \sum_{k=1}^{\infty} k b_k x^{k-1}.$$

From this we obtain the following recurrence relation

$$(10.14) \qquad (k+1)a_{k+1} = b_1 a_k + 2b_2 a_{k-1} + 3b_3 a_{k-2} + \ldots + k b_k a_1 \,, \qquad k \geq 1,$$

with $a_0 = 1$.

Taking for b_k the coefficients of (6.19) viz.

$$b_k = \frac{B_{k+1}}{k(k+1)} \,,$$

we obtain

$$(10.15) \qquad (k+1)a_{k+1} + \tfrac{1}{2}B_2 a_k + \tfrac{1}{4}B_4 a_{k-2} + \ldots \,.$$

A simple calculation shows that

$$a_0 = 1 \qquad\qquad a_3 = -\frac{139}{51840}$$

$$a_1 = \frac{1}{12} \qquad\qquad a_4 = -\frac{571}{2488320} \,.$$

$$a_2 = \frac{1}{288}$$

Thus we finally obtain

$$(10.16) \qquad \omega! = \omega^{\omega+\frac{1}{2}} \, e^{-\omega} \, \sqrt{2\pi} \, \{1 + \frac{1}{12\omega} + \frac{1}{288\omega^2} - \frac{139}{51840\omega^3} -$$

$$- \frac{571}{2488320\omega^4} + O(\omega^{-5})\}.$$

11. THE SADDLE POINT METHOD

We consider the asymptotic behaviour of a function $f(\omega)$ of the following kind

$$(11.1) \qquad f(\omega) = \int_C e^{-\omega\phi(z)} \psi(z)dz \quad , \qquad\qquad \omega \to \infty$$

where $\phi(z)$ and $\psi(z)$ are analytic functions of the complex variable z and where C is a certain path in the complex z-plane. As usual it is assumed that ω is a real and positive variable which tends to plus infinity.

The idea of the saddle point method is briefly to deform the path C in such a way that the integral expression becomes equivalent to that of the real case (9.11).

However, before explaining the method in detail we recall a few well-known facts from the theory of complex analytic functions.
We write

$$(11.2) \qquad \phi(z) = h(x,y) + ik(x,y) \quad , \qquad\qquad z = x + iy$$

where h and k are the real and the imaginary part respectively. Then we have the Cauchy-Riemann equations

$$\frac{\partial h}{\partial x} = \frac{\partial k}{\partial y} \quad , \qquad \frac{\partial h}{\partial y} = -\frac{\partial k}{\partial x} .$$

The functions $h(x,y)$ and $k(x,y)$ are so-called conjugate harmonic functions satisfying the potential equation

$$\Delta h = \Delta k = 0.$$

If $h(x,y)$ is given, then $k(x,y)$ is determined up to an arbitrary additive constant. In terms of hydrodynamic potential flow the lines h = constant may be called potential lines and the lines k = constant stream lines. Each set is the set of orthogonal trajectories of the other set.

Of great importance are the points with $\phi'(z) = 0$. They correspond to the stagnation points of the hydrodynamic flow where the velocity becomes zero. In such a point we have

$$\frac{\partial h}{\partial x} = \frac{\partial h}{\partial y} = \frac{\partial k}{\partial x} = \frac{\partial k}{\partial y} = 0.$$

At a stagnation point the potential function $h(x,y)$ and the stream function $k(x,y)$ are stationary and may take a local maximum or minimum value on a line through this point.

Next we consider the properties of the analytic function

(11.3) $F(z) = \exp - \phi(z)$.

The absolute value of $F(z)$ defines the modular landscape

(11.4) $|F(z)| = \exp - h(x,y)$.

The potential lines $h(x,y)$ = constant are the level lines of the landscape. The stream lines $k(x,y)$ = constant are the orthogonal trajectories of the level lines and may be called lines of steepest descent (or ascent). Along such a line $F(z)$ has a constant phase since

(11.5) $\arg F(z) = - k(x,y)$.

The stagnation points of $\phi(z)$ are the saddles or passes of the modular landscape. The landscape determined by (11.4) cannot have local extrema since a harmonic function has no internal extrema in its domain. Therefore the only stationary points of $|F(z)|$, the points with a horizontal tangent plane, are saddles.

If $F'(z_0) = 0$ but $F''(z_0) \neq 0$, we have an ordinary saddle. If also $F''(z_0) = 0$, we have a higher order saddle. If e.g. $F'''(z_0) \neq 0$, the saddle is sometimes called a monkey saddle (two legs and one tail).

Example 11.1

For $\phi(z) = z^2$ the landscape $|F| = \exp(y^2-x^2)$ has a saddle at $x = y = 0$. The level curves are hyperbolas $x^2 - y^2$ = constant. The steepest descent curves are hyperbolas xy = constant. The level curves through the saddle are the straight lines $x \pm y = 0$. They separate the highland $y^2 > x^2$ from the lowland $y^2 < x^2$. The steepest descent lines through the saddle are the lines $x = 0$ and $y = 0$. The situation is sketched in fig. 11.1.

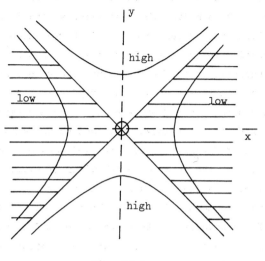

fig. 11.1

Example 11.2

For $\phi(z) = z^3$ the landscape $|F| = \exp(-x^3 + 3xy^2)$ has a monkey saddle at $x = y = 0$. The level curves are third-order hyperbolas $x(3y^2 - x^2) = $ constant. The level curves through the saddle are the straight lines $x = 0$, $y = \pm\ x$ tg30°. The steepest descent lines through the saddle are the lines Im $z^3 = 0$ or $y = 0$, $y = \pm\ x$ tg60°. The situation is sketched in fig.11.2.

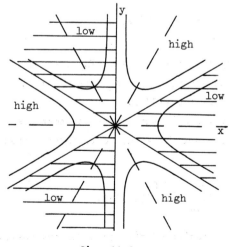

fig. 11.2

After these preliminaries we consider now the asymptotic properties
of (11.1). In order to simplify the discussion we shall neglect for the
moment the function $\psi(z)$ by taking $\psi(z) \equiv 1$. Furthermore we assume that
$\phi(z)$ is of algebraic kind so that it is analytic throughout the z-plane
and its only singularities are branch points and poles. For simplicity we
take a path C that starts and ends with $h(x,y) = \infty$. Then C is deformed
into a steepest descent line of exp - $h(x,y)$. The new path passes through
the valleys and reaches its highest positions at the saddles of $\phi(z)$.
Along the new path of integration all contributions of the integrand are
in equal phase so that the asymptotic behaviour of (11.1) is essentially
that of the real case (9.11). It is clear that for $\omega \to \infty$ the asymptotic
behaviour of $f(\omega)$ is determined only by the behaviour of $\phi(z)$ in the
neighbourhood of the saddles. If there are more saddles on this line of
steepest descent each saddle makes its own contribution but we may take
into consideration only those saddles for which $h(x,y)$ takes on a maximum
value.

If $\psi(z)$ is added to the picture, we may have a variety of complica-
tions. The deformation of C into the steepest descent path may involve
the crossing of one or more poles or singularities of $\psi(z)$, or even worse
a saddle of ϕ may coincide with a singularity of ψ.

Example 11.3

We consider the integral

$$f(\omega) = \int_{-\infty}^{\infty} e^{-\omega(z^2 - 2zi)} \psi(z)dz.$$

There is a single saddle point at z = i. The steepest descent curves are
$x(y-1)$ = constant. The steepest descent line y = 1 passes through the
valleys and goes through the saddle.
The contour $C(-\infty,\infty)$ may be shifted to the steepest descent line Im z = 1.
If $\psi(z)$ is sufficiently well-behaved, the integral expression can be written
as

$$f(\omega) = e^{-\omega} \int_{-\infty}^{\infty} e^{-\omega t^2} \psi(i+t)dt.$$

The full asymptotic expansion of $f(\omega)$ then follows easily from the expansion of $\psi(i+t)$ in powers of t. The first term is

$$f(\omega) \sim \pi^{\frac{1}{2}}\psi(i)\omega^{-\frac{1}{2}}e^{-\omega}.$$

If, however, $\psi(z)$ has a single pole z_0 in the strip $0 \le \mathrm{Im}\ z \le 1$, we have to add the residue at the pole. If $\psi(z) = \dfrac{1}{z-z_0} + \ldots$ this means a contribution

$$2\pi i\ \exp\ -\omega(z_0^2 - 2z_0 i).$$

Depending on the position of z_0 the one or the other term dominates.

Example 11.4

The partial differential equation

$$\frac{\partial^2 f}{\partial x^2} + \frac{\partial^2 f}{\partial y^2} - \omega^2 f = 0 \qquad , \qquad \omega > 0,$$

has the general solution

$$f(x,y,\omega) = \int_C \exp\ -\omega(x\ \cosh\ w - iy\ \sinh\ w)\ \psi(w)dw,$$

where C starts at $-\infty + ia$ and ends at $\infty + ib$. The saddle points are determined by $x\ \sinh\ \omega = iy\ \cosh\ \omega$. Writing $x + iy = r\ \exp\ i\theta$, we find $\sinh(\omega - i\theta) = 0$. This gives a sequence of saddles $\omega = i(\theta + n\pi)$ where n is an integer. The steepest descent lines are determined by $\sinh\ u\ \sin(v-\theta) = $ constant where $w = u + iv$. We consider in particular the general solution for $a = b = 0$ with a sufficiently well-behaved function $\psi(w)$. Then the integral converges in the halfplane $x > 0$, i.e. for $-\frac{1}{2}\pi < \theta < \frac{1}{2}\pi$. The saddle which is nearest to C is $w = i\theta$. The steepest descent line through this saddle is the line $v = \theta$. It is easy to see that $C(v=0)$ may be shifted to the position $v = \theta$ without violating the conditions at infinity for the convergence of the integral. Substitution of $w = i\theta + u$ gives

$$f(x,y,\omega) = \int_{-\infty}^{\infty} e^{-\omega r\ \cosh\ u}\psi(i\theta + u)du$$

so that asymptotically

$$f(x,y,\omega) \sim \left(\frac{2\pi}{\omega r}\right)^{\frac{1}{2}}\psi(i\theta)e^{-\omega r}.$$

Example 11.5

We consider the integral

$$f(\omega) = \int_C \exp -\omega(z^2+2/z)dz,$$

where C is the line Im z = a (a>0) with increasing Re z.
The origin is an essential singularity.
There are three saddles : 1, $-\frac{1}{2} \pm \frac{1}{2}i\sqrt{3}$. The steepest descent lines are
determined by $xy - y(x^2+y^2)^{-1}$ = constant. The lines which pass through
the saddles z = 1 and z =k(= $-\frac{1}{2} + \frac{1}{2}i\sqrt{3}$) are sketched in fig.11.3.

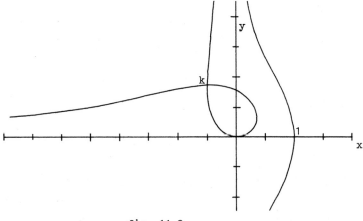

fig. 11.3

They are respectively given by y = 0, $x(x^2+y^2)$ = 1 and by $(xy+\frac{3}{4}\sqrt{3})$.
(x^2+y^2) = y.
Looking for the valley parts the ideal path of integration is found to be
as sketched in fig.11.4

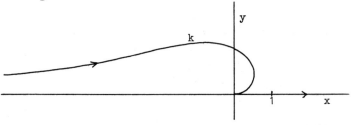

fig. 11.4

The height of the landscape $|\exp - \omega(z^2+2/z)|$ at the saddles 1 and k is
respectively exp - 3ω and exp$\frac{3}{2}\omega$. Therefore only the latter saddle has to

be taken into account for obtaining the required asymptotic behaviour.
The steepest descent direction at z = k is determined by

$$z^2 + 2/z = 3k^2 + 3(z-k)^2 + \dots .$$

Thus the steepest descent direction at z = k for the valleys is horizontal.
The effort spent in an accurate quantitative determination of the steepest
descent line of fig.11.4 is almost of no use,since the only thing that
matters is the local behaviour at the dominating saddle point at z = k.
If one is interested only in the main term of the asymptotic expansion of
f(ω),it suffices to make the local transformation at z = k viz.

$$z = k + t$$

where t is real. This gives

$$f(\omega) \sim \exp\ (\tfrac{3}{2} + i\tfrac{3\sqrt{3}}{2})\omega \int_{-\infty}^{\infty} e^{-3\omega t^2} dt$$

or finally

$$f(\omega) \sim (\tfrac{\pi}{3\omega})^{\tfrac{1}{2}} \exp\ (\tfrac{3}{2} + i\tfrac{3\sqrt{3}}{2})\omega.$$

The following general and systematic treatment is due to van der
Waerden [19]. In this treatment it is easily possible to deal with more
complicated situations such as the coincidence of a saddle point with a
singularity. Van der Waerden's method will be presented here in a rather
formal way. It is, however, not difficult to make all analytic steps completely rigoureus,merely by stating the necessary restrictive conditions
at the beginnning. Again we consider the integral expression (11.1) for
large positive values of ω. For simplicity it is assumed that at both ends
of C the real part of $\phi(z)$ tends to plus infinity.

Van der Waerden's method consists of studying the complex transformation

$$w = \phi(z) \qquad , \qquad w = u + iv.$$

We note that by this transformation the steepest descent lines and the

level curves of exp - ωφ(z) are transformed into the horizontal and vertical coördinate lines of the (u,v)-plane.

The transformation is singular at the saddles of φ(z). Any point where
φ'(z) = 0 gives rise to a branch point and a corresponding branch line
in the complex w-plane. This holds of course for saddles of any order.
By this map the path C is transformed into a contour C' which meanders
between branch points and poles in the w-plane.

We may now write

$$(11.6) \qquad f(\omega) = \int_{C'} e^{-\omega w} \psi\{z(w)\} \frac{dz}{dw} dw.$$

A typical situation is sketched in fig.11.5.

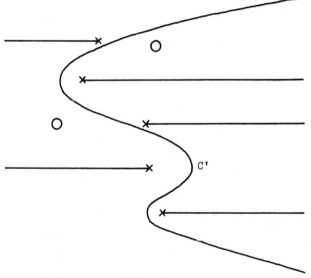

fig. 11.5

Apart from the branch points and poles due to the factor dz/dw there may
be similar singularities due to the factor $\psi\{z(w)\}$.

The idea of the saddle point method is to transform the contour C' in
such a way that

$$|\exp - \omega w| = \exp - \omega u$$

becomes as small as possible on the contour. This means that C' should be shifted to the right as far as possible. It is clear that the best form of the contour in this sense consists of loops surrounding the branch points and poles, coming from infinity in straight lines from the right and going back to infinity along the same lines straight to the right as shown in fig.11.6

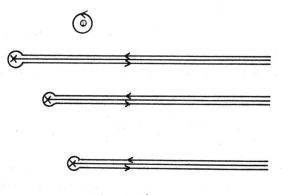

fig. 11.6

It is equally clear that only the branch point (or points) at the leftmost position contributes to the asymptotic behaviour of $f(\omega)$.

Let us assume for simplicity that we are left with a single branch point at $w = 0$. If this is a branch point of the order two, we may perform the local substitution $s = w^{\frac{1}{2}}$. Then the integrand function

$$(11.7) \qquad F(w) = \psi\{z(w)\}dz/dw$$

has a pole at $s = 0$ of the first order and admits an expansion of the kind

$$(11.8) \qquad F(w) = a_{-1}s^{-1} + a_0 + a_1 s + \ldots .$$

This gives

$$f(\omega) = 2 \int_{-\infty}^{\infty} e^{-\omega s^2} (a_{-1}+a_0 s+a_1 s^2+\ldots)ds,$$

so that

$$(11.9) \qquad f(\omega) \sim \left(\frac{\pi}{\omega}\right)^{\frac{1}{2}} \left(2a_{-1} + \frac{a_1}{\omega} + \ldots\right).$$

If w = 0 is a branch point of order three, we may use the local uniformi-
zing substitution $s = w^{1/3}$. With due regard to the interpretation of $F(w)$
at the upper and the lower side of the branch cut we have, again with the
expansion (11.8),

$$f(\omega) = 3 \int_{C''} e^{-\omega s^3} (a_{-1}s + a_0 s^2 + a_1 s^3 + \ldots) ds,$$

where C'' consists of two of the three rays in the complex s-plane
$\arg s = 0, \pm \frac{2}{3}\pi$.
If the ray with $\arg s = 0$ does not contribute, we find after a simple calculation

(11.10) $$f(\omega) \sim \frac{-i\ 3^{\frac{1}{2}}\ \Gamma(2/3)}{\omega^{2/3}} a_{-1} + \frac{i\ 3^{\frac{1}{2}}\ \Gamma(4/3)}{\omega^{4/3}} a_1 + \ldots .$$

If w = 0 is a branch point of the order two and at the same time a pole
of the first order, there are no special difficulties. Instead of (11.8)
we have an expansion

(11.11) $$F(w) = a_{-2}s^{-2} + a_{-1}s^{-1} + a_0 + \ldots .$$

The contribution of the first term to the asymptotic expansion becomes

$$\int a_{-2} w^{-1} dw = -2i\pi a_{-2}.$$

Example 11.6

We consider anew the function $f(\omega)$ of the previous example. We now perform
the complex transformation

$$w = z^2 + 2/z.$$

This map has branch points in the w-plane at $w = 3$ and $w = \frac{3}{2} \pm \frac{3}{2}i\sqrt{3}$.
Taking for the path of integration C the line $\text{Im } z = \frac{1}{2}$, we obtain in the
w-plane a contour C' as sketched in fig.11.7 together with the branch
cuts.

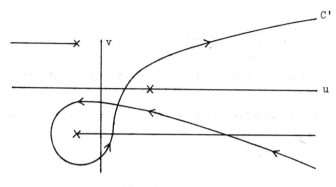

fig. 11.7

The asymptotic behaviour of $f(\omega)$ is determined only by the branch point at $-\frac{3}{2} - \frac{3}{2}i\sqrt{3}$. The contribution of the branch point at $w = 3$ is asymptotically negligible. Thus we have

$$f(\omega) \sim \int_{C''} e^{-\omega w} dz/dw \ dw,$$

where C'' is formed by the upper and lower sides of the branch cut at $w = -\frac{3}{2} - \frac{3}{2}i\sqrt{3}$. If the map $z \to w$ is combined with the local transformation

$$w = -\frac{3}{2} - \frac{3}{2}i\sqrt{3} + s^2$$

we have, with the short-hand notation $k = -\frac{1}{2} + \frac{1}{2}i\sqrt{3}$,

$$s^2 = -3k^2 + z^2 + 2/z.$$

Inversion gives

$$z = k + \frac{s}{\sqrt{3}} + \frac{k^2}{9}s^2 + \dots \ .$$

Thus we obtain at last

$$f(\omega) \sim e^{-3k^2\omega} \int_{-\infty}^{\infty} e^{-\omega s^2} (\frac{1}{\sqrt{3}} + \frac{2k^2}{9}s + \dots)ds \ ,$$

which leads to the final result of the previous example.

Example 11.7

We consider the integral

$$f(\omega) = \int_{-\infty}^{\infty} e^{-\omega(z^2-2zi)}(z^2+1)^{-1}dz .$$

There is a complication due to the coincidence of the saddle $z = i$ with a pole.
According to the general theory we may perform at once the transformation

$$z^2 - 2zi = 1 + s^2 ,$$

which, however, is nothing more than

$$z = i + s.$$

With this substitution $f(\omega)$ becomes

$$f(\omega) = e^{-\omega} \int_{C''} e^{-\omega s^2} \{\frac{1}{2is} + \frac{1}{4} + \ldots\}ds$$

where C'' is the real axis with an indentation below the pole $s = 0$.
We easily find

$$f(\omega) \sim e^{-\omega}(\tfrac{1}{2}\pi + \tfrac{1}{4}(\tfrac{\pi}{\omega})^{\frac{1}{2}} + \ldots).$$

12. THE ASYMPTOTIC BEHAVIOUR OF COEFFICIENTS OF A POWER SERIES

Sometimes one is faced by the problem of considering the asymptotic behaviour of the coefficient a_n of a power series expansion

$$(12.1) \qquad f(z) = \sum_{n=0}^{\infty} a_n z^n$$

of an analytic function for $n \to \infty$.
The obvious starting point is the Cauchy formula

$$(12.2) \qquad a_n = \frac{1}{2\pi i} \oint z^{-n-1} f(z)dz .$$

If we make the complex transformation $z = \exp w$, an expression is obtained to which the saddle point method may be applied. In many cases, however, a more direct - but essentially equivalent - method is available. Its principle is, briefly, to move the contour in (12.2) away from the origin as far as possible. The method works smoothly for functions of algebraic growth at infinity with a finite number of poles and branch points. Then the ideal contour consists of small circles around the poles and straight lines along branch cuts radiating away from the origin. The situation for $f(z) = (z^3+1)^{\frac{1}{2}} (z-1)^{-1}$ is sketched below by way of illustration.

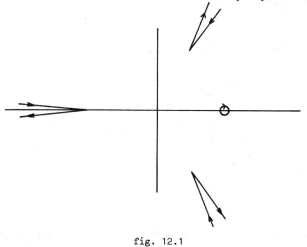

fig. 12.1

However, if $f(z)$ has an essential singularity at $z = \infty$ the simple method illustrated in the following examples cannot be followed. An example of such a case will be considered in chapter 18 where a Hermite polynomial is defined as a coefficient of a certain power series.

Example 12.1

For $f(z) = (1-z)^{-\frac{1}{2}}$ we have the well-known expression

$$a_n = \frac{1.3. \dots (2n-1)}{2.4.6 \dots 2n} \, .$$

According to (12.2) we have

$$a_n = \frac{1}{2\pi i} \int_C z^{-n-1}(1-z)^{-\frac{1}{2}} dz \, .$$

For C we take the upper and lower side of the branch cut at the positive real axis from 1 to ∞. Putting $z = \exp t$, we obtain

$$a_n = \frac{e^{\frac{1}{2}\pi i} - e^{-\frac{1}{2}\pi i}}{2\pi i} \int_0^\infty e^{-nt}(e^t - 1)^{-\frac{1}{2}} dt \, ,$$

or

$$a_n = \frac{1}{\pi} \int_0^\infty e^{-nt} t^{-\frac{1}{2}} \psi(t) dt \, ,$$

where

$$\psi(t) = \left(\frac{e^t - 1}{t}\right)^{-\frac{1}{2}} \, .$$

Applying theorem 6.4 we find without difficulty

$$a_n \sim \frac{1}{\pi} \sum_{k=0}^\infty c_k \frac{(k-\frac{1}{2})!}{n^{k+\frac{1}{2}}} \, ,$$

where c_k are the coefficients in the expansion of $\psi(t)$. Explicitly

$$a_n \sim \frac{1}{\sqrt{\pi n}} \left(1 - \frac{1}{8n} + \dots\right).$$

Example 12.2

The Legendre polynomials $P_n(x)$ are the coefficients of the generating function $(1-2xz+z^2)^{-\frac{1}{2}}$. Then the Cauchy formula gives

$$P_n(\cos \theta) = \frac{1}{2\pi i} \oint z^{-n-1}(e^{i\theta} - z)^{-\frac{1}{2}}(e^{-i\theta} - z)^{-\frac{1}{2}} dz \, .$$

There are branch points at $z = \exp \pm i\theta$.

For the contribution from the branch cut at $z = \exp i\theta$ we obtain

$$\frac{e^{-\frac{1}{2}i\theta}}{\pi} \int_0^\infty e^{-n(t+i\theta)} (e^t-1)^{-\frac{1}{2}} (e^{-i\theta}-e^{i\theta+t})^{-\frac{1}{2}} dt =$$

$$= \frac{1}{\pi}(-2i \sin \theta)^{-\frac{1}{2}} e^{-(n+\frac{1}{2})i\theta} \int_0^\infty e^{-nt} t^{-\frac{1}{2}} \{1+0(t)\} dt =$$

$$= (2n\pi \sin \theta)^{-\frac{1}{2}} e^{-(n+\frac{1}{2})i\theta+\frac{1}{4}i\pi} \{1+0(n^{-1})\}.$$

Since the contribution from the second branch cut is conjugate complex, it suffices to take twice the real part. In this way we obtain at last

$$P_n(\cos \theta) = (\tfrac{1}{2}n\pi \sin \theta)^{-\frac{1}{2}} \cos\{(n+\tfrac{1}{2})\theta-\tfrac{1}{4}\pi\} + 0(n^{-3/2}),$$

valid for $0 < \theta < \pi$.

13. THE ASYMPTOTIC EXPANSION OF THE GAMMA AND RELATED FUNCTIONS

The AE of the factorial function z! has no simple structure. A related function with a simpler explicit AE is the digamma function or psi function (6.11) or

(13.1) $\qquad \psi(z) = d \log \Gamma(z)/dz$.

The simplicity of the AE of $\psi(z)$ is due to the fact that $\psi(z+1) - \log z$ is the Laplace transform of a rather elementary function. According to (6.13) we have for Re z > 0

(13.2) $\qquad \psi(z+1) - \log z = \int_0^\infty e^{-zt}(\frac{1}{t} - \frac{1}{e^t-1})dt$.

The AE of $\psi(z+1)$ as obtained in section 6 as formula (6.14) becomes

(13.3) $\qquad \psi(z+1) - \log z \sim \frac{1}{2z} - \sum_{k=1} \frac{B_{2k}}{2k} z^{-2k}$, $\quad |arg\ z| < \pi$.

We quote the related AE (6.16)

(13.4) $\qquad \psi(z+a) - \psi(z) \sim \sum_{k=1} (-1)^{k-1} \frac{B_k(a) - B_k}{k} z^{-k}$.

Explicitly we have

(13.5) $\qquad \psi(z+1) \sim \log\ z + \frac{1}{2z} - \frac{1}{12z^2} + \frac{1}{120z^4} - \frac{1}{252z^6} + \cdots$,

and

(13.6) $\qquad \psi(z+a) - \psi(z) \sim \frac{a}{z} - \frac{a^2-a}{2z^2} + \frac{2a^3-3a^2+a}{6z^3} - \cdots$.

The AE of log z! is almost equally simple. According to (6.19) we have

(13.7) $\qquad \log\ z! \sim (z+\frac{1}{2})\log\ z - z + \frac{1}{2}\log\ 2\pi + \sum_{k=1} \frac{B_{2k}}{2k(2k-1)} z^{-2k+1}$,

for $|arg\ z| < \pi$.

Explicitly

(13.8) $\log z! \sim (z+\tfrac{1}{2}) \log z - z + \tfrac{1}{2}\log 2\pi + \dfrac{1}{12z} - \dfrac{1}{360z^3} + \dfrac{1}{1260z^5} - \ldots$.

The AE of z! is obtained from this by taking the exponential

(13.9) $z! \sim e^{-z}z^{z+\frac{1}{2}}\sqrt{2\pi} \displaystyle\sum_{k=0} a_k z^{-k}$,

where

$$a_0 = 1 \;,\; a_1 = \frac{1}{12} \;,\; a_2 = \frac{1}{288} \;,\; a_3 = -\frac{139}{51840} \;,\; \ldots$$

There is no simple explicit expression for these coefficients, neither is there a simple recurrence relation. However, in example 10.1 it is shown that

(13.10) $a_k = 2^k(\tfrac{1}{2})_k(2k+1)d_{2k+1}$, $k = 0,1,\ldots$,

where the coefficients d_k are given by the power series

(13.11) $t = \displaystyle\sum_{k=1}^{\infty} d_k u^k$, $d_1 = 1$,

where

(3.13) $t - \log(1+t) = \tfrac{1}{2}u^2$.

In some applications one needs the AE of functions such as $(z+a)!/z!$ or $z!/(z-a)!$. The AE follows from (13.6) or (13.9) by elementary calculations. A more direct way is by using some integral representation of Euler's betafunction. In this way, cf. example 6.6, we may obtain the result

(13.13) $\dfrac{(z+a)!}{(z+b)!} \sim z^{a-b}\{1+\tfrac{1}{2}(a-b)(a+b+1)z^{-1}+O(z^{-2})\}$.

Similar results are

(13.14) $\dfrac{(z+a)!}{z!} \sim z^a\{1+\tfrac{1}{2}(a^2+a)z^{-1}+\tfrac{1}{24}(3a^4+2a^3-3a^2-2a)z^{-2}+\ldots\}$,

$$(13.15) \qquad \frac{z!}{(z-a)!} \sim z^a \{1 - \tfrac{1}{2}(a^2-a)z^{-1} + \tfrac{1}{24}(3a^4 - 10a^3 + 9a^2 - 2a)z^{-2} + \ldots\}.$$

The incomplete gammafunction $\Gamma(a,z)$ is defined by

$$(13.16) \qquad \Gamma(a,z) = \int_z^\infty e^{-t} t^{a-1} dt \quad , \qquad \text{Re } a > 0.$$

The AE for $z \to \infty$ can easily be obtained from the corresponding Laplace representation

$$(13.17) \qquad \Gamma(a,z) = z^a e^{-z} \int_0^\infty e^{-zt}(1+t)^{a-1} dt$$

by using theorem 6.4. By rotating the line of integration the result can be extended to all arguments within $(-\pi,\pi)$. The result is

$$(13.18) \qquad \Gamma(a,z) \sim z^{a-1} e^{-z} \sum_{k=0} \frac{(a-1)(a-2)\ldots(a-k)}{z^k} .$$

The special case $a = 0$ has already been discussed in section 4 (formula 4.17) and in section 7 (example 7.3), where the divergent APS has been transformed into a convergent factorial series. The same trick may be applied in the general case. The representation (13.17) can be brought in the following form

$$(13.19) \qquad \Gamma(a,z) = z^a e^{-z} \int_0^1 (1-t)^{z-1} \phi(t) dt ,$$

with

$$\phi(t) = \{1 - \log(1-t)\}^{a-1} = \sum_{k=0} b_k t^k.$$

Then from theorem 7.7 we obtain at once

$$(13.20) \qquad \Gamma(a,z) = z^{a-1} e^{-z} \sum_{k=0}^\infty \frac{k! b_k}{(z+1)\ldots(z+k)} .$$

The first few coefficients are

$$b_0 = 1 \quad , \quad b_1 = a - 1 \quad , \quad b_2 = \tfrac{1}{2}(a-1)^2 \quad , \quad \ldots .$$

The factorial series converges for all z with Re $z > 0$. At the same time it is an AE in the sector $|\arg z| < \pi$.

Also the second method of section 7 leads to a relatively simple convergent AE. Starting again from (13.17) we may write

$$(1+t)^a = \sum_{k=0}^{\infty} \frac{(a)_k}{k!} \left(\frac{t}{1+t}\right)^k .$$

Substitution gives at once

$$(13.21) \qquad \Gamma(a,z) = z^{a-1} e^{-z} \sum_{k=0}^{\infty} \frac{(a)_k}{k!} s_k(z) ,$$

where $s_k(z)$ is defined by (7.27). In view of the asymptotic behaviour (7.29) convergence is established outside the negative real axis.

14. THE ASYMPTOTIC EXPANSION OF BESSEL FUNCTIONS FOR A LARGE ARGUMENT

The Bessel functions are defined as properly normalized solutions
of Bessel's differential equation

$$(14.1) \qquad \frac{d^2 f}{dz^2} + \frac{1}{z} \frac{df}{dz} + (1 - \frac{\nu^2}{z^2}) f = 0.$$

The standard solution is taken to be

$$(14.2) \qquad J_\nu(z) = \sum_{k=0}^{\infty} \frac{(-1)^k}{k!(k+\nu)!} (\tfrac{1}{2}z)^{\nu+2k} ,$$

a power series expansion valid for all values of z. A second independent
solution of (14.1) is $J_{-\nu}(z)$ unless ν is an integer. If n is a (non-nega-
tive) integer, then

$$(14.3) \qquad J_{-n}(z) = (-1)^n J_n(z).$$

However, Neumann's function, defined as

$$(14.4) \qquad Y_\nu(z) = \frac{\cos \nu\pi \, J_\nu(z) - J_{-\nu}(z)}{\sin \nu\pi} ,$$

is always independent of $J_\nu(z)$.
It turns out that for integer order $J_n(z)$ is an entire function and that
$Y_n(z)$ has a logarithmic singularity at z = 0.
In particular

$$(14.5) \qquad J_0(z) = \sum_{k=0}^{\infty} \frac{(-1)^k}{k!k!} (\tfrac{1}{4}z^2)^k ,$$

$$(14.6) \qquad Y_0(z) = \frac{2}{\pi} J_0(z) \log \tfrac{1}{2}z - \frac{2}{\pi} \sum_{k=0}^{\infty} \frac{(-1)^k \psi(k+1)}{k!k!} (\tfrac{1}{4}z^2)^k ,$$

where (cf. formula 6.11)

$$\psi(k+1) = -\gamma + 1 + \tfrac{1}{2} + \dots + \frac{1}{k} .$$

The standard pair $J_\nu(z)$, $Y_\nu(z)$ is adapted to their behaviour at the origin.
However, it is not the simplest pair with respect to their asymptotic behaviour. Then the Hankel functions are preferable.

These are defined as

(14.7)
$$H_\nu^{(1)}(z) = J_\nu(z) + iY_\nu(z) ,$$
$$H_\nu^{(2)}(z) = J_\nu(z) - iY_\nu(z) .$$

A similar situation occurs in the theory of the trigonometric functions, which are the solutions of the differential equation $f'' + f = 0$. The standard pair is $\cos z$, $\sin z$ but with respect to the asymptotic behaviour we may better take the pair $\exp \pm iz = \cos z \pm i \sin z$.

The modified Bessel functions are defined as solutions of the equation

(14.8)
$$\frac{d^2 f}{dz^2} + \frac{1}{z}\frac{df}{dz} - (1 + \frac{\nu^2}{z^2})f = 0,$$

which follows from (14.1) by changing z into iz.
An obvious standard solution is

(14.9)
$$I_\nu(z) = \sum_{k=0}^{\infty} \frac{1}{k!\,(k+\nu)!} (\tfrac{1}{2}z)^{\nu+2k}$$

so that

(14.10)
$$I_\nu(z) = i^{-\nu} J_\nu(iz) .$$

The second independent solution, however, is not derived from the Neumann function but from the Hankel function

(14.11)
$$K_\nu(z) = \tfrac{1}{2}\pi i \; e^{\frac{1}{2}\nu\pi i} H_\nu^{(1)}(iz) .$$

It can be derived from (14.4) and (14.7) that

(14.12)
$$K_\nu(z) = \tfrac{1}{2}\pi \frac{I_{-\nu}(z) - I_\nu(z)}{\sin \nu\pi} .$$

This shows that $K_\nu(z)$ is real for real z and real ν and further that

(14.13
$$K_{-\nu}(z) = K_\nu(z) .$$

84

Continuing the trigonometric analogy, we may compare the pair $I_\nu(z)$, $K_\nu(z)$ to cosh z and exp - z. In fact, one of the attractive properties of $K_\nu(z)$ is its exponentially vanishing behaviour at positive infinity.

Before tackling the asymptotic behaviour of the various Bessel functions we consider a few typical cases. We take $\nu = 0$ and $z = \omega$ real and positive. The asymptotic behaviour of $J_0(\omega)$ can be derived from an integral representation. The simplest is

$$(14.14) \qquad J_0(\omega) = \frac{1}{\pi} \int_0^\pi \cos(\omega \sin t)dt.$$

The integral may be written in a form which permits application of the saddle point technique

$$J_0(\omega) = \frac{1}{2\pi i} \int_{-i\pi}^{i\pi} e^{-\omega \sinh w}dw.$$

The path may be supplemented by adding a piece Im w = $-\pi$, $-\infty <$ Re w < 0 and a piece Im w = π, $-\infty <$ Re w < 0 as shown in figure 14.1. In view of the periodicity $2\pi i$ of sinh w the net contribution is zero so that

$$(14.15) \qquad J_0(\omega) = \frac{1}{2\pi i} \int_L e^{-\omega \sinh w}dw \, ,$$

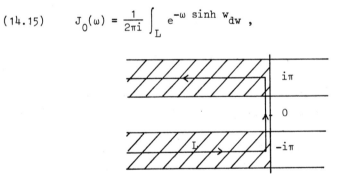

fig. 14.1

where L is a contour equivalent to the one shown in figure 14.1. Writing w = u + iv the convergence of the integral at u → $-\infty$ requires that cos v < 0. This means that L starts at u = $-\infty$ in the strip $-\frac{3}{2}\pi <$ v < $-\frac{1}{2}\pi$ and ends at u = $-\infty$ in the strip $\frac{1}{2}\pi <$ v < $\frac{3}{2}\pi$. The saddle points follow from cosh w = 0. This gives the two possibilities w = $\pm \frac{1}{2}\pi i$. The steepest descent path L_- through $-\frac{1}{2}\pi i$ is determined by

$$\cosh u \sin v = -1.$$

This path starts at $-\infty - \pi i$, passes through the saddle $-\frac{1}{2}\pi i$ in the direction $\frac{1}{4}\pi$ and ends at $+\infty - 0i$ as shown in fig. 14.2.

The steepest descent path L_+ through $\frac{1}{2}\pi i$ is determined by

$$\cosh u \sin v = +1,$$

and is the mirror image of the former path with respect to the real axis (see fig.14.2).

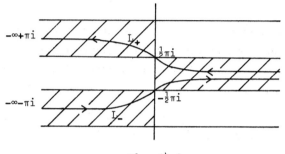

fig. 14.2

For the contribution of the lower path we make the substitution

(14.16) $\sinh w = -i + 2s^2$,

so that L_- in the s-plane is transformed into the real axis. Locally at the saddle this means

$$w = -\frac{1}{2}\pi i + 2s\sqrt{i} + O(s^3).$$

A simple calculation shows that

$$\frac{1}{2\pi i} \int_{L_-} e^{-\omega \sinh w} dw = \frac{e^{i\omega}}{\pi\sqrt{i}} \int_{-\infty}^{\infty} e^{-2\omega s^2} \frac{ds}{\sqrt{1+is^2}} .$$

The AE now follows at once by expanding the integrand function

(14.17) $(1+is^2)^{-\frac{1}{2}} = \sum_{k=0}^{\infty} \frac{(-i)^k (\frac{1}{2})_k}{k!} s^{2k} .$

The result is

$$(14.18) \qquad (2\pi\omega)^{-\frac{1}{2}} e^{i(\omega-\frac{1}{4}\pi)} \sum_{k=0}^{\infty} \frac{(\frac{1}{2})_k (\frac{1}{2})_k}{k!(2\omega i)^k} .$$

The contribution of the upper path L_+ gives the complex conjugate. Summing up we find

$$(14.19) \qquad J_0(\omega) \sim (\frac{2}{\pi\omega})^{\frac{1}{2}} \sum_{k=0}^{\infty} \frac{(\frac{1}{2})_k (\frac{1}{2})_k}{k!} \frac{\cos(\omega-\frac{1}{4}\pi-\frac{1}{2}k\pi)}{(2\omega)^k} .$$

The asymptotic expansion of $I_0(\omega)$ can be obtained, as has been shown in example 6.4 (cf. formula 6.10), in a much simpler way.
The starting point is the same integral representation (14.14), but now written as

$$(14.20) \qquad I_0(\omega) = \frac{1}{\pi} \int_{-1}^{1} e^{-\omega t}(1-t^2)^{-\frac{1}{2}} dt = \frac{e^\omega}{\pi} \int_{0}^{2} e^{-\omega t}(2t-t^2)^{-\frac{1}{2}} dt.$$

We repeat the result

$$(14.21) \qquad I_0(\omega) \sim (\frac{1}{2\pi\omega})^{\frac{1}{2}} e^\omega \sum_{k=0}^{\infty} \frac{(\frac{1}{2})_k (\frac{1}{2})_k}{k!(2\omega)^k} .$$

The asymptotic expansion of $K_0(\omega)$ can be obtained from a similar integral representation

$$(14.22) \qquad K_0(\omega) = \int_{1}^{\infty} e^{-\omega t}(t^2-1)^{-\frac{1}{2}} dt = e^{-\omega} \int_{0}^{\infty} e^{-\omega t}(2t+t^2)^{-\frac{1}{2}} dt.$$

Theorem 6.4 gives at once

$$(14.23) \qquad K_0(\omega) \sim (\frac{\pi}{2\omega})^{\frac{1}{2}} e^{-\omega} \sum_{k=0}^{\infty} \frac{(-1)^k (\frac{1}{2})_k (\frac{1}{2})_k}{k!(2\omega)^k} .$$

It may come somewhat as a surprise that also the product $I_0(\omega)K_0(\omega)$ admits a rather simple asymptotic expansion. Although its AE can be obtained from (14.21) and (14.23) by multiplication we may better use the integral representation

$$(14.24) \qquad I_0(\omega)K_0(\omega) = \int_{0}^{\infty} e^{-\omega^2 t} \frac{1}{2t} I_0(\frac{1}{2t}) e^{-\frac{1}{2t}} dt.$$

Substituting the AE (14.21) in the integrand and applying theorem 6.4, we find without difficulty

$$(14.25) \qquad I_0(\omega)K_0(\omega) \sim \frac{1}{2\omega} \sum_{k=0} \frac{(\tfrac{1}{2})_k (\tfrac{1}{2})_k (\tfrac{1}{2})_k}{k!\,\omega^{2k}} .$$

The asymptotic expansions of the Bessel functions in the general case can be obtained from the so-called Sommerfeld integral representations of the Hankel functions

$$(14.26) \qquad H_\nu^{(j)}(z) = \frac{1}{\pi i} \int_{L_j} \exp(-z \sinh w + \nu w)\,dw,$$

where for $j = 1$ and $j = 2$ the path of integration L_j in the complex w-plane is as given in fig.14.3 with $\theta = \arg z$.

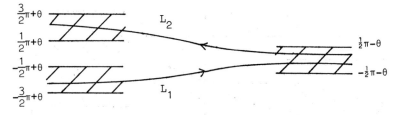

In order to simplify the analysis we shall consider only Bessel functions with a real order ν. It is, however, possible to extend the results to complex values of ν since the Hankel functions are entire functions with respect to the complex variable ν. The hatched regions in fig.14.3 indicate where the integrals converge with respect to Re $w \to \pm \infty$. Writing $w = u + iv$, convergence requires Re $z \sinh w \to \infty$ or

$$e^u \cos(v+\theta) - e^{-u} \cos(v-\theta) \to \infty$$

Between the two Hankel functions there exists the following relation

$$(14.27) \qquad H_\nu^{(2)}(z) = -e^{i\nu\pi} H_\nu^{(1)}(e^{i\pi}z),$$

which is a simple consequence of the representation (14.26). Therefore we may restrict our discussion to the first Hankel function only.

Taking $j = 1$ and $z = \omega \exp i\theta$, $\omega > 0$ in (14.26), we see that the integral representation is of the kind (11.1) with

$$\phi(w) = e^{i\theta} \sinh w \quad , \quad \psi(w) = \frac{1}{\pi i} e^{vw} .$$

The only relevant saddle point is $w = -\frac{1}{2}\pi i$. The corresponding steepest descent path is given by

(14.28) $e^u \sin(v+\theta) + e^{-u} \sin(v-\theta) = -2 \cos \theta.$

By way of illustration this path is sketched in fig.14.4 for the special case $\theta = \frac{1}{4}\pi$.

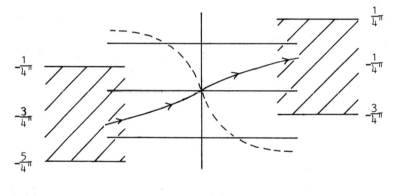

fig. 14.4

The part of the steepest descent line which passes through the valleys is drawn in full. It is obvious that for this special case the contour L_1 can be deformed into this steepest descent line through the saddle. It is not difficult to recognize this possibility for all values of θ in the interval $(-\pi, 2\pi)$.

Following the technique used for the special case (14.15), we again perform the transformation $w \to s$ of (14.16), but with a minor alteration (14.29) $\sinh w = -i(1+2s^2)$. A simple calculation shows that

(14.30) $H_\nu^{(1)}(z) = \frac{2}{\pi i} \exp i(z-\tfrac{1}{2}\nu\pi) \int e^{2is^2 z} \frac{(s+\sqrt{1+s^2})^{2\nu}}{\sqrt{1+s^2}} ds ,$

where the path of integration is the straight line

$$s = t \exp i(\tfrac{1}{4}\pi - \tfrac{1}{2}\theta),$$

with t running from minus infinity to plus infinity. The AE now follows by using the power series expansion

(14.31)
$$(1+s^2)^{-\tfrac{1}{2}}(s+\sqrt{1+s^2})^{2\nu} = \sum_{k=0}^{\infty} a_k s^k.$$

The Cauchy formula gives

$$a_k = \frac{1}{2\pi i} \oint \frac{(s+\sqrt{1+s^2})^{2\nu}}{s^{k+1}\sqrt{1+s^2}}ds = \frac{1}{2\pi i} \oint e^{2\nu z}(\sinh z)^{-k-1}dz.$$

Partial integration gives the recurrence relation

$$k(k-1)a_k = \{4\nu^2 - (k-1)^2\}a_{k-2}.$$

Starting from $a_0 = 1$ we obtain

(14.32)
$$(2k)!a_{2k} = (4\nu^2-1^2)(4\nu^2-3^2) \ldots (4\nu^2-(2k-1)^2) .$$

The final result is

(14.33)
$$H_\nu^{(1)}(z) \sim (\frac{2}{\pi z})^{\tfrac{1}{2}} e^{i(z-\tfrac{1}{2}\nu\pi-\tfrac{1}{4}\pi)} .$$

$$. \sum_{k=0}^{\infty} \frac{(1/4-\nu^2)(9/4-\nu^2)\ldots\{(k-\tfrac{1}{2})^2-\nu^2\}}{k!(2iz)^k}$$

valid for $-\pi < \arg z < 2\pi$.

The relation (14.27) gives the corresponding expansion of the second Hankel function

(14.34)
$$H_\nu^{(2)}(z) \sim (\frac{2}{\pi z})^{\tfrac{1}{2}} e^{-i(z-\tfrac{1}{2}\nu\pi-\tfrac{1}{4}\pi)} .$$

$$. \sum_{k=0}^{\infty} \frac{(1/4-\nu^2)(9/4-\nu^2)\ldots\{(k-\tfrac{1}{2})^2-\nu^2\}}{k!(-2iz)^k}$$

valid for $-2\pi < \arg z < \pi$.

The relations (14.7) next give the AE of $J_\nu(z)$ and $Y_\nu(z)$. For $J_\nu(z)$ we find

$$(14.35) \qquad J_\nu(z) \sim \left(\frac{2}{\pi z}\right)^{\frac{1}{2}} \sum_{k=0}^{\infty} \frac{(1/4-\nu^2)(9/4-\nu^2)\ldots\{(k-\frac{1}{2})^2-\nu^2\}}{k!(2z)^k} \, .$$

$$\cdot \cos\{z-\tfrac{1}{2}(\nu+k+\tfrac{1}{2})\pi\} \, ,$$

which holds in the strip $-\pi < \arg z < \pi$.

However, in the upper half of this strip, i.e. for $0 < \arg z < \pi$, the asymptotic behaviour of $H_\nu^{(1)}(z)$ is asymptotically negligible with respect to that of $H_\nu^{(2)}(z)$ whereas at the lower half, i.e. for $-\pi < \arg z < 0$ the opposite is true. This means explicitly that

$$J_\nu(z) \sim \tfrac{1}{2}H_\nu^{(2)}(z) \sim \left(\frac{1}{2\pi z}\right)^{\frac{1}{2}} e^{-i(z-\frac{1}{2}\nu\pi-\frac{1}{4}\pi)}(1+\ldots),$$

for $\mathrm{Im}\, z > 0$,
and

$$J_\nu(z) \sim \tfrac{1}{2}H_\nu^{(1)}(z) \sim \left(\frac{1}{2\pi z}\right)^{\frac{1}{2}} e^{i(z-\frac{1}{2}\nu\pi-\frac{1}{4}\pi)}(1+\ldots),$$

for $\mathrm{Im}\, z < 0$.

The fact that the same function is represented by different asymptotic expressions in different regions of the complex plane, is a phenomenon which is often observed in asymptotics. Usually this is called Stokes' phenomenon due to Stokes who first drew attention to this singular behaviour which contradicts the continuation of analytic functions. The line $\mathrm{Im}\, z = 0$ where both regions meet is usually called a Stokes line.

15. AIRY FUNCTIONS

The Airy functions are solutions of the so-called Airy equation

(15.1) $$\frac{d^2 f}{dz^2} - zf = 0.$$

A straightforward calculation shows that by the transformation $f \to z^{\frac{1}{2}}f$, $z \to (\frac{3}{2}z)^{2/3}$ the Airy equation passes into the modified Bessel equation (14.8) with $\nu = \pm 1/3$. Thus (15.1) has the independent solutions

$$z^{\frac{1}{2}} I_{\frac{1}{3}}(\tfrac{2}{3}z^{3/2}) \qquad , \qquad z^{\frac{1}{2}} I_{-\frac{1}{3}}(\tfrac{2}{3}z^{3/2})$$

or

$$z^{\frac{1}{2}} I_{\frac{1}{3}}(\tfrac{2}{3}z^{3/2}) \qquad , \qquad z^{\frac{1}{2}} K_{\frac{1}{3}}(\tfrac{2}{3}z^{3/2}).$$

The Airy functions $Ai(z)$ and $Bi(z)$ are defined as

(15.2) $$Ai(z) = \frac{1}{\pi}(\tfrac{z}{3})^{\frac{1}{2}}\, K_{\frac{1}{3}}(\tfrac{2}{3}z^{3/2}) \,,$$

(15.3) $$Bi(z) = (\tfrac{z}{3})^{\frac{1}{2}}\, \{I_{-\frac{1}{3}}(\tfrac{2}{3}z^{3/2}) + I_{\frac{1}{3}}(\tfrac{2}{3}z^{3/2})\}.$$

These definitions show that all properties of the Airy functions can be deduced from the theory of the Bessel functions. However, their occurrence in problems of mathematical physics and asymptotics justifies an independent treatment. The definitions (15.2) and (15.3) tend to obscure the basic simple properties of the Airy functions. They are entire functions of z with a singular behaviour at infinity, which makes them interesting at a level just beyond the exponential and trigonometric functions. Equation (15.1) is one of the simplest equations in which a so-called turning point occurs. Both $Ai(x)$ and $Bi(x)$ for real x are exponential for $x > 0$ and oscillatory for $x < 0$ (see fig.15.1).

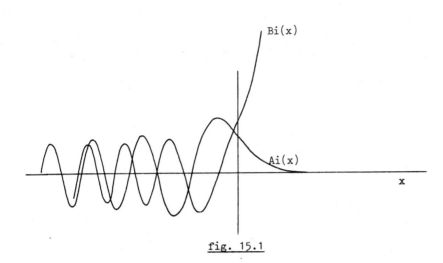

<u>fig. 15.1</u>

Substitution of a power series expansion $f = \sum a_k z^k$ in (15.1) easily leads
to the two independent possibilities

$$f_1 = 1 + \frac{z^3}{2.3} + \frac{z^6}{2.3.5.6} + \frac{z^9}{2.3.5.6.8.9} + \cdots ,$$

(15.4)

$$f_2 = z + \frac{z^4}{3.4} + \frac{z^7}{3.4.6.7} + \frac{z^{10}}{3.4.6.7.9.10} + \cdots .$$

For the Airy functions they are combined as follows

(15.5) $\qquad Ai(z) = \frac{3^{-2/3}}{(-1/3)!} f_1 - \frac{3^{-1/3}}{(-2/3)!} f_2 ,$

(15.6) $\qquad Bi(z) = \frac{3^{-1/6}}{(-1/3)!} f_1 + \frac{3^{1/6}}{(-2/3)!} f_2 .$

The Airy functions arose in 1838 when Airy studied mathematical op-
tics. Originally, the first Airy function was for real x defined as the
Airy integral

(15.7) $\qquad Ai(x) = \frac{1}{\pi} \int_0^\infty \cos(\frac{1}{3}t^3 + xt) dt .$

This representation cannot be used for complex arguments. However, it is
easily seen that the integral

(15.8) $\qquad \dfrac{1}{2\pi i}\displaystyle\int_{L} \exp(\tfrac{1}{3}w^{3}-zw)dw$,

where L is a path as shown in figure 15.2,

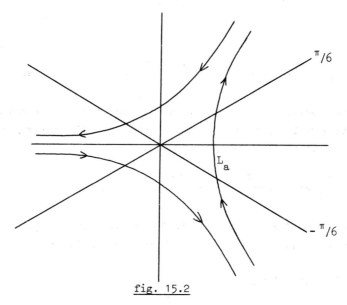

fig. 15.2

is a solution of (15.1). It is seen that L starts at infinity where Re $w^{3} < 0$ and ends at infinity in a different sector with the same condition. The path indicated as L_{a} clearly gives the integral representation of Ai(z).

The asymptotic behaviour of the Airy function follows at once from that of the modified Bessel functions when we use the definitions (15.2) and (15.3). The results are as follows

(15.9) $\qquad Ai(z) \sim \tfrac{1}{2}\pi^{-\frac{1}{2}}z^{-\frac{1}{4}} \exp(- \tfrac{2}{3}z^{3/2})(1 - \tfrac{5}{48}z^{-3/2} + \ldots)$,

valid for $\qquad |\arg z| < \pi$,

(15.10) $\qquad Bi(z) \sim \pi^{-\frac{1}{2}}z^{-\frac{1}{4}} \exp(\tfrac{2}{3}z^{3/2})(1 + \tfrac{5}{48}z^{-3/2} + \ldots)$,

valid for $\qquad |\arg z| < \tfrac{1}{3}\pi$.

These results may be supplemented by

(15.11) $Ai(-z) \sim \pi^{-\frac{1}{2}} z^{-\frac{1}{4}} \sin(\frac{\pi}{4} + \frac{2}{3}z^{3/2})$, $|arg\ z| < \frac{2}{3}\pi$,

and

(15.12) $Bi(-z) \sim \pi^{-\frac{1}{2}} z^{-\frac{1}{4}} \cos(\frac{\pi}{4} + \frac{2}{3}z^{3/2})$, $|arg\ z| < \frac{2}{3}\pi$.

It may be instructive to show how these asymptotic results can be derived in a more direct way from the representation (15.8). If $z = x$ real and positive, we write (15.8) as

$$Ai(x) = \frac{x^{\frac{1}{2}}}{2\pi i} \int_{L_a} e^{-x^{3/2}(w-\frac{1}{3}w^3)} dw .$$

The relevant saddle point is $w = 1$. The steepest descent path follows from $Im\ (w-\frac{1}{3}w^3) = 0$ as a hyperbolic branch satisfying, with $w = u + iv$,

$$u^2 - \frac{1}{3}v^2 = 1.$$

Following the standard procedure, we perform the transformation

$$w - \frac{1}{3}w^3 = \frac{2}{3} - s^2$$

with the local behaviour

$$w - 1 = s - \frac{1}{6}s^2 + \dots .$$

This gives

$$Ai(x) = x^{\frac{1}{2}} \exp(- \frac{2}{3}x^{3/2}) \frac{1}{2\pi i} \int_{-i\infty}^{i\infty} e^{x^{3/2}s^2} \frac{dw}{ds} ds.$$

The technical problem of expanding dw/ds in a power series $\sum a_k s^k$ can be solved by using Cauchy's formula. Considering coefficients with an even index only, since coefficients with an odd index do not contribute to the expansion of $Ai(x)$, we have

$$a_{2k} = \frac{1}{2\pi i} \oint \frac{dw}{s^{2k+1}} = \frac{3^{k+\frac{1}{2}}}{2\pi i} \oint \frac{dw}{\{(w-1)^2(2+w)\}^{k+\frac{1}{2}}} ,$$

where w describes a small circle around w = 1. The latter representation can be rewritten as

$$a_{2k} = \frac{1}{2\pi i} \oint \frac{(1+\frac{1}{3}z)^{-k-\frac{1}{2}}dz}{z^{2k+1}} ,$$

where z describes a circle around the origin. The right-hand side represents the coefficient of z^{2k} in the power series expansion of $(1+\frac{1}{3}z)^{-k-\frac{1}{2}}$. Thus we have

$$a_{2k} = \frac{(k+\frac{1}{2})_{2k}}{3^{2k}(2k)!} .$$

Straightforward calculations eventually lead to the final result

(15.13) $$Ai(x) \sim \tfrac{1}{2}\pi^{-\frac{1}{2}}x^{-\frac{1}{4}}e^{-\xi} \sum_{k=0} \frac{(-1)^k(k+\frac{1}{2})_{2k}}{k!(54\xi)^k} ,$$

where

$$\xi = \frac{2}{3}x^{3/2} .$$

Airy functions often occur in connection with first order nonlinear differential equations such as

(15.14) $$\frac{df}{dx} + f^2 = x.$$

Indeed, by putting f = g'/g this equation passes into Airy's equation (15.1). The general solution of (15.14) can then be written as

(15.15) $$f(x) = \frac{Ai'(x)+cBi'(x)}{Ai(x)+cBi(x)} .$$

It can be derived from (15.9) and (15.10) that for $x \to \infty$

(15.16) $$f(x) \sim x^{\frac{1}{2}}$$ provided c ≠ 0.

On the other hand for c = 0 we have

(15.17) $$\frac{Ai'(x)}{Ai(x)} \sim -x^{\frac{1}{2}} - \frac{1}{4x} + \frac{5}{32x^{5/2}} + \dots .$$

The coefficients of the asymptotic series on the right-hand side should
not be obtained from (15.13) and the similar expansion of Ai'(x), but
directly from (15.14) by substituting the formal series

$$(15.18) \qquad f = \pm\, x^{\frac{1}{2}}(1 + \sum_{k=1} a_k\, x^{-3k/2}).$$

The corresponding result for the Bi(x) function becomes

$$(15.19) \qquad \frac{Bi'(x)}{Bi(x)} \sim x^{\frac{1}{2}} - \frac{1}{4x} - \frac{5}{32x^{5/2}} + \dots\; .$$

16. BESSEL FUNCTIONS OF LARGE ORDER AND LARGE ARGUMENT

In this section we shall consider what happens if in the Bessel function $J_\nu(z)$ both ν and z are large. For reasons of simplicity it will be assumed that both ν and z are real and positive. Accordingly we shall write x instead of z. From (14.26) we may derive the following fundamental formula

$$(16.1) \qquad J_\nu(x) = \frac{1}{2\pi i} \int_L \exp(-x \sinh w + \nu w)dw,$$

where the path of integration is as sketched in fig. 16.1.

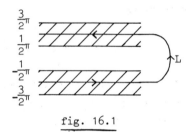

fig. 16.1

Saddle points follow from

$$(16.2) \qquad \cosh w = \nu/x.$$

This leads to the following three cases

1. $\qquad \nu < x.$

We write $\nu = \omega$ and $x = \omega/\cos \alpha$, with $0 < \alpha < \frac{1}{2}\pi$. The saddle points are given by

$$(16.3) \qquad w = \pm\, i\alpha + 2in\pi \quad (n=0,\pm1,\ldots).$$

2. $\qquad \nu > x.$

We write $\nu = \omega$ and $x = \omega/\cosh \beta$ with $\beta > 0$. The saddle points are given by

$$(16.4) \qquad w = \pm\, \beta + 2in\pi \quad (n=0,\pm1,\ldots).$$

98

3. $\nu = x$.

Writing $\nu = x = \omega$, we obtain a third order saddle point at $w = 0$ and further a series of ordinary saddle points on the imaginary axis

(16.5) $w = 0$ (twice), $w = 2in\pi$ ($n=0,\pm1,\ldots$).

    Starting with the first case $\nu < x$, we observe that the asymptotic be-
haviour is determined by both saddle points $w = \pm i\alpha$, the contributions of
which are complex conjugate. Thus it suffices to consider only the saddle
point $i\alpha$ and to take twice the real part of its contribution afterwards. A
local expansion at $w = i\alpha$ gives

(16.6) $\sinh w/\cos \alpha - w = i(tg\alpha-\alpha) + \tfrac{1}{2}i\ tg\alpha(w-i\alpha)^2 + \ldots .$

We shall restrict the discussion to the leading term of the asymptotic expansion. Then the contribution from the upper saddle point can be written
down at once, without further substitutions, as

(16.7) $- \exp\{-i\omega(tg\alpha-\alpha)\}\ \dfrac{1}{2\pi i} \displaystyle\int \exp\{-\tfrac{1}{2}i\omega\ tg\alpha(w-i\alpha)^2\}dw,$

where w follows the tangent line $w = i\alpha + t \exp - \tfrac{1}{4}\pi i$ at $i\alpha$. Thus we obtain

(16.8) $(2\pi\omega\ tg\alpha)^{-\frac{1}{2}} \exp - i\{\omega(tg\alpha-\alpha)-\tfrac{1}{4}\pi\}.$

By taking twice the real part we obtain finally

(16.9) $J_\omega(\omega/\cos \alpha) \sim (\dfrac{2}{\pi\omega\ tg\alpha})^{\frac{1}{2}} \cos\{\omega(tg\alpha-\alpha)-\tfrac{1}{4}\pi\}.$

The asymptotic approximation breaks down for $\alpha \to 0$, i.e., when $\nu/x \to 1$.
In fact this necessitates the separate discussion of a further case, when
ν and x are both large and approximately equal. We shall, however, take
the second case next.
    The asymptotic behaviour for the second case requires an investiga-
tion at the two saddle points $w = \pm \beta$. The appropriate contribution comes
from $w = -\beta$. The local expansion is

(16.10) $\sinh w/\cosh \beta - w = (\beta-\tanh \beta) - \tfrac{1}{2} \tanh \beta(w+\beta)^2 + \ldots .$

The leading term of the asymptotic expansion is therefore

$$(16.11) \qquad \exp\{-\omega(\beta-\tanh \beta)\} \frac{1}{2\pi i} \int \exp\{\tfrac{1}{2}\omega \tanh \beta(w+\beta)^2\}dw,$$

where w follows the vertical tangent line $w = -\beta + it$. The final result is

$$(16.12) \qquad J_\omega(\omega/\cosh \beta) \sim (\frac{1}{2\pi\omega \tanh \beta})^{\tfrac{1}{2}} \exp\{-\omega(\beta-\tanh \beta)\}.$$

Again this approximation breaks down for $\beta \to 0$, i.e. when $\nu/x \to 1$.

The difficulties at the line $\nu = x$ in the (ν,x)-plane are an illustration of the Stokes' phenomenon. We shall now discuss the case $\nu \approx x$ in more detail.

Writing $\nu = \omega$ and $x = \omega + c$, we have

$$(16.13) \qquad J_\omega(\omega+c) = \frac{1}{2\pi i} \int_L e^{-\omega(\sinh w-w)} \exp(-c \sinh w)dw.$$

The asymptotic behaviour is now determined by the third-order saddle point at $w = 0$. Although it is not necessary to know the steepest descent path explicitly we give it here for sake of completeness. Its equation is

$$(16.14) \qquad \cosh u \sin v = v$$

which is illustrated in fig. 16.2.

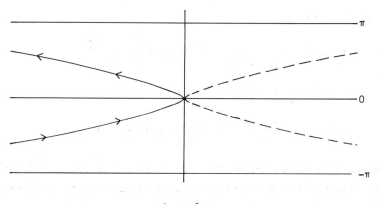

fig. 16.2

By means of the complex transformation

$$(16.15) \qquad \sinh w - w = \frac{1}{6} s^3,$$

the steepest descent path is automatically changed in the pair of lines
$\arg s = \pm \frac{2}{3} \pi$.
The inverse of (16.15) is

$$(16.16) \qquad w = s - \frac{1}{60} s^3 + \frac{1}{1400} s^5 + \dots \ .$$

A simple calculation shows that

$$(16.17) \qquad e^{-c} \sinh w \frac{dw}{ds} = \sum_{k=0}^{\infty} c_k s^k,$$

with

$$c_0 = 1 \qquad\qquad c_3 = -\frac{1}{6} c^3 - \frac{1}{10} c$$

$$c_1 = -c \qquad\qquad c_4 = \frac{1}{24} c^4 + \frac{1}{8} c^2 + \frac{1}{280} \ .$$

$$c_2 = \tfrac{1}{2} c^2 - \frac{1}{20}$$

Then we have

$$(16.18) \qquad J_\omega(\omega + c) = \frac{1}{\pi} \operatorname{Im} \int_0^\infty e^{\exp \frac{2}{3}\pi i - \frac{1}{6}\omega s^3} \sum_{k=0}^{\infty} c_k s^k \, ds$$

so that asymptotically

$$(16.19) \qquad J_\omega(\omega + c) \sim \frac{1}{3\pi} \sum_{k=0}^{\infty} c_k \Gamma(\tfrac{k+1}{3}) \sin \tfrac{2k+2}{3}\pi \left(\tfrac{6}{\omega}\right)^{\frac{k+1}{3}}.$$

The first few terms are

$$(16.20) \qquad J_\omega(\omega + c) \sim \frac{1}{2\pi\sqrt{3}} \left(\tfrac{6}{\omega}\right)^{1/3} \{\Gamma(\tfrac{1}{3}) + c\Gamma(\tfrac{2}{3}) \left(\tfrac{6}{\omega}\right)^{1/3} + \dots\}.$$

Again complications arise if $|c|$ is large and of order $\omega^{1/3}$, for then
the asymptotic series looses its asymptotic character. It is, however, not
difficult to cover also this exceptional case. We shall write

(16.21) $\nu = 2\omega$, $x = 2\omega + \gamma\omega^{1/3}$,

where γ is either a positive or a negative constant. Performing the same transformation (16.15), we may bring (16.13) into the following form

(16.22) $J_{2\omega}(2\omega+\gamma\omega^{1/3}) = \dfrac{1}{2\pi i} \int e^{-1/3\omega s^3 - \gamma\omega^{1/3}s} F(s)ds$,

where

(16.23) $F(s) = \exp\{\gamma\omega^{1/3}(s-\sinh w)\}dw/ds$,

and where s follows the two lines arg $s = \pm \dfrac{2}{3}\pi$.
As in (16.17) we may expand $F(s)$ as

(16.24) $F(s) = \sum\limits_{k=0}^{\infty} \gamma_k(\omega)s^k$,

with

$$\gamma_0 = 1 \qquad\qquad \gamma_3 = -\dfrac{3}{20}\gamma\omega^{1/3}$$
$$\gamma_1 = 0 \qquad\qquad \gamma_4 = \dfrac{1}{280} \; .$$
$$\gamma_2 = -\dfrac{1}{20}$$

We note that generally $\gamma_k = O(\omega^{k/9})$. Then we have

(16.25) $J_{2\omega}(2\omega+\gamma\omega^{1/3}) \sim \sum\limits_{k=0}^{\infty} \gamma_k \, \omega^{-\frac{k+1}{3}} L_k(\gamma)$,

where the functions $L_k(\gamma)$ are defined as

(16.26) $L_k(\gamma) = \dfrac{1}{2\pi i} \int s^k \exp - (\tfrac{1}{3}s^3+\gamma s)ds$.

The net gain at each term of this asymptotic series is of the order $\omega^{-2/9}$.
It follows from (15.8) that $L_0(\gamma)$ is related to the Airy function. In fact, by changing s into $-s$ it is easily seen that

(16.27) $L_0(\gamma) = Ai(-\gamma)$,

and next

(16.28) $L_k(\gamma) = Ai^{(k)}(-\gamma)$.

Thus the dominating term of (16.25) gives

(16.29) $J_{2\omega}(2\omega-\gamma\omega^{1/3}) = \dfrac{Ai(\gamma)}{\omega^{1/3}} + O(\omega^{-1})$.

By this asymptotic formula the transitional behaviour is exhibited in an
explicit way. For $\gamma > 0$ we have an exponential decline with respect to γ.
For $\gamma < 0$ we have an oscillatory behaviour with respect to γ.

We end this section by discussing briefly a related AE which, however,
is of a simpler kind. We consider $I_\nu(x)$ for both a and ν large. From
(14.10) and (16.1) we have the integral representation

(16.30) $I_\nu(x) = \dfrac{1}{2\pi i} \displaystyle\int \exp(x \cosh w + \nu w)dw$,

where the path is that of fig.16.3.
We write $\nu = \omega$ and $\sinh a = \nu/x$.
The saddle points are determined by

$$\sinh w + \sinh a = 0,$$

but it is easily seen that $w = -a$ is the only relevant saddle. The steepest
descent path follows from

$$\sinh u \sin v + v \sinh a = 0$$

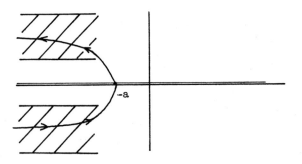

fig. 16.3

as the curved path of fig. 16.3. The path $v = 0$, however, goes uphill and cannot be used.

The local behaviour at the saddle point

$$x \cosh w + w = (x \cosh a - a) + \tfrac{1}{2}x \cosh a (w+a)^2 + \ldots$$

suffices to obtain the dominant term of the AE.

In fact, we have

$$I_\nu(x) \sim \exp(x \cosh a - \nu a) \frac{1}{2\pi i} \int_{-i\infty}^{i\infty} \exp(\tfrac{1}{2}s^2 x \cosh a)\,ds,$$

so that

(16.31) $$I_\nu(x) \sim (2\pi x \cosh a)^{-\frac{1}{2}} \exp(x \cosh a - \nu a),$$

where

$$x \cosh a = \sqrt{\nu^2 + x^2} \quad , \quad a = \ln \frac{\nu + \sqrt{\nu^2 + x^2}}{x} \, .$$

17. CONFLUENT HYPERGEOMETRIC FUNCTIONS

The function of Kummer $M(a,c,z)$ is derived from the hypergeometric function $F(a,b,c,z)$ in the following way

$$(17.1) \qquad M(a,c,z) = \lim_{b \to \infty} F(a,b,c,z/b).$$

This limit process can be described as a confluence of two singularities, viz. b and ∞, of the hypergeometric function $F(a,b,c,z/b)$. Therefore $M(a,c,z)$ is also called a confluent hypergeometric function. From the well-known properties of the hypergeometric function it can be derived that Kummer's function has the power series expansion

$$(17.2) \qquad M(a,c,z) = \sum_{k=0}^{\infty} \frac{(a)_k z^k}{(c)_k \, k!},$$

and that it satisfies the differential equation

$$(17.3) \qquad z \frac{d^2 f}{dz^2} + (c-z)\frac{df}{dz} - af = 0,$$

also called Kummer's differential equation.
The expansion (17.2) converges for all values of a, c and z with $c \neq 0,-1,-2,\ldots$.
If c is not integer, a second independent solution of (17.3) is given by $z^{1-c} M(a-c+1,2-c,z)$, so that the general solution of Kummer's equation, a confluent hypergeometric function, can be represented by

$$(17.4) \qquad A M(a,c,z) + Bz^{1-c} M(a-c+1,2-c,z).$$

If c is a positive integer, by a proper limit process a second independent solution can be derived in a similar way as for Bessel functions of integer order.

The starting point for obtaining asymptotic expansions is a suitable integral representation. We may try to solve (17.3) by an integral of the kind

$$(17.5) \qquad f(z) = \int_C e^{zs} \psi(s)ds,$$

where C is an open or closed contour.

Substitution gives

(17.6) $\psi(s) = s^{a-1}(s-1)^{c-a-1}$,

where C is either a closed contour or a path such that $s^a(s-1)^{c-a}$ exp zs vanishes at the endpoints. The simplest case is

(17.7) $M(a,c,z) = \dfrac{\Gamma(c)}{\Gamma(a)\Gamma(c-a)} \displaystyle\int_0^1 e^{zt}\, t^{a-1}(1-t)^{c-a-1}dt$,

valid for Re c > Re a > 0 and all z.

The domain of validity can be extended by analytic continuation with respect to c and a.

If the variable of integration t is replaced by 1 − t, we obtain the following functional relation

(17.8) $M(a,c,z) = e^z\, M(c-a,c,-z)$.

The next case is

(17.9) $M(a,c,z) = \dfrac{\Gamma(c)\Gamma(a-c+1)}{\Gamma(a)}\ \dfrac{1}{2\pi i} \displaystyle\int_0^{(1^+)} e^{zs}\, s^{a-1}\, (s-1)^{c-a-1}ds$,

valid for Re a > 0.

The representations (17.7) and (17.9) are easy to prove. In both cases the right-hand side is a solution of (17.3) and represents an entire function of z. There remains to check the value M = 1 for z = 0.

Both representations can be used to obtain the AE of $M(a,c,z)$ for $z \to \infty$ with either $|\arg z| < \tfrac{1}{2}\pi$ or $|\arg -z| < \tfrac{1}{2}\pi$, by applying theorem 6.4. It is sufficient to consider only $|\arg z| < \tfrac{1}{2}\pi$, since by (17.8) the AE is obtained for the other half-plane. If we take the more general representation (17.9), we expand $s^{a-1}(s-1)^{c-a-1}$ in powers of s − 1. By integrating the resulting series we obtain

(17.10) $M(a,c,z) \sim \dfrac{\Gamma(c)}{\Gamma(a)}\ e^z\, z^{a-c}\ \displaystyle\sum_{k=0}^{\infty} \dfrac{(c-a)_k(1-a)_k}{k!}\ z^{-k}$,

valid for $|\arg z| < \tfrac{1}{2}\pi$.

From (17.8) we obtain

$$(17.11) \qquad M(a,c,z) \sim \frac{\Gamma(c)}{\Gamma(c-a)} (-z)^{-a} \sum_{k=0}^{\infty} \frac{(a)_k (a-c+1)_k}{k!} z^{-k},$$

valid for $|\arg -z| < \frac{1}{2}\pi$.

These expansions are derived still with the restriction Re a > 0. However, the domain of validity can be extended by using the difference relation

$$(17.12) \qquad M(a-1,c,z) = M(a,c,z) - \frac{z}{c} M(a,c+1,z).$$

Thus (17.10) and (17.11) appear to hold for all values of a and c, with the possible exception of c = 0, -1, -2, ...

The general confluent hypergeometric function (17.4) has for $|\arg z| < \frac{1}{2}\pi$ the AE

$$(17.13) \qquad f \sim (A\frac{\Gamma(c)}{\Gamma(a)} + B\frac{\Gamma(2-c)}{\Gamma(a-c+1)}) e^z z^{a-c} \sum_{k=0}^{\infty} \frac{(c-a)_k (1-a)_k}{k!} z^{-k}.$$

For a certain combination of A and B this expansion vanishes. This suggests the existence of a solution of (17.3) with an asymptotic behaviour of lower order.
Such a solution is given by the following integral representation, another example of (17.5),

$$(17.14) \qquad U(a,c,z) = \frac{1}{\Gamma(a)} \int_0^{\infty} e^{-zt} t^{a-1} (1+t)^{c-a-1} dt,$$

valid for Re a > 0 and Re z > 0,
or more generally

$$(17.15) \qquad U(a,c,z) = \frac{\Gamma(1-a)}{2\pi i} \int^{(0^+)} e^{zs} s^{a-1} (1-s)^{c-a-1} ds,$$

where for Re z > 0 the contour starts at $\infty \exp - i\pi$, encircles the origin in the positive direction and ends at $\infty \exp i\pi$. The region of validity can be extended by rotating the path of integration.
In this way U(a,c,z) is defined by (17.15) for $|\arg z| < \frac{3}{2}\pi$.
The AE of (17.15) is obtained by expanding $(1-s)^{c-a-1}$ in powers of s. The result is

$$(17.16) \qquad U(a,c,z) \sim z^{-a} \sum_{k=0} \frac{(a)_k (a-c+1)_k}{k!} (-z)^{-k},$$

valid for $|\arg z| < \frac{3}{2}\pi$.

With $U(a,c,z)$, also $z^{1-c} U(a-c+1,2-c,z)$ is a solution of (17.3). However, since both solutions have the same AE, they must be identical. Therefore we have the relation

$$(17.17) \qquad U(a,c,z) = z^{1-c} U(a-c+1,2-c,z).$$

The secondary solution of (17.3) $U(a,c,z)$ is of the form (17.13), with constants A and B determined by the vanishing of (17.13) and by its behaviour
at $z = 0$. The explicit result is

$$(17.18) \qquad U(a,c,z) = \frac{\Gamma(1-c)}{\Gamma(a-c+1)} M(a,c,z) + \frac{\Gamma(c-1)}{\Gamma(a)} z^{1-c} M(a-c+1,2-c,z).$$

On the other hand, for $U(a,c,z)$ a functional relation of the kind (17.8)
does not hold. But

$$e^z U(c-a,c,e^{+i\pi} z)$$

is again a solution of Kummer's equation. Since this solution has a different asymptotic behaviour it is independent of $U(a,c,z)$. This means that
$M(a,c,z)$ can be written as a linear combination of both functions. Taking
into account the known behaviour at $z = 0$ and at $z = \infty$, we find

$$(17.19) \quad M(a,c,z) = \frac{\Gamma(c)}{\Gamma(c-a)} e^{i\pi a} U(a,c,z) + \frac{\Gamma(c)}{\Gamma(a)} e^{i\pi(a-c)} e^z U(c-a,c,e^{-i\pi}z),$$

valid for $\operatorname{Im} z > 0$, and a similar relation with $i \to -i$ for $\operatorname{Im} z < 0$.
Using (17.19) with the AE (17.16) we find a more detailed asymptotic ex-
pression which combines (17.10) and (17.11).

A great number of special functions may be considered as special cases
of the confluent hypergeometric functions. We list a few only:

exponential function

$$(17.20) \qquad M(a,a,z) = e^z,$$

incomplete gamma function

(17.21) $U(1-a,1-a,z) = e^z \Gamma(a,z),$

error functions

(17.22) $M(\frac{1}{2},3/2,-z^2) = \frac{\sqrt{\pi}}{2z} \text{ erf } z,$

(17.23) $U(\frac{1}{2},\frac{1}{2},z^2) = \sqrt{\pi} \, e^{z^2} \text{ erfc } z,$

Bessel functions

(17.24) $M(\nu+\frac{1}{2},2\nu+1,2z) = \nu! \, e^z \, (\frac{1}{2}z)^{-\nu} \, I_\nu(z),$

(17.25) $U(\nu+\frac{1}{2},2\nu+1,2z) = \pi^{-\frac{1}{2}} \, e^z \, (2z)^{-\nu} \, K_\nu(z).$

Closely related to the confluent hypergeometric functions are the Whittaker functions, which are properly normalized solutions of Whittaker's differential equation

(17.26) $\dfrac{d^2 f}{dz^2} + (-\frac{1}{4} + \dfrac{k}{z} + \dfrac{\frac{1}{4}-m^2}{z^2})f = 0.$

The definitions are

(17.27) $W_{k,m}(z) = e^{-\frac{1}{2}z} \, z^{\frac{1}{2}+m} \, U(\frac{1}{2}+m-k,1+2m,z),$

and

(17.28) $M_{k,m}(z) = e^{-\frac{1}{2}z} \, z^{\frac{1}{2}+m} \, M(\frac{1}{2}+m-k,1+2m,z).$

The functions $M_{k,m}(z)$ and $M_{k,-m}(z)$ constitute a set of independent solutions of (17.26). However,

$$W_{k,m}(z) = W_{k,-m}(z).$$

In fact, from (17.18) we obtain

(17.27) $W_{k,m}(z) = \dfrac{\Gamma(2m)}{\Gamma(\frac{1}{2}+m-k)} M_{k,-m}(z) + \dfrac{\Gamma(-2m)}{\Gamma(\frac{1}{2}-m-k)} M_{k,m}(z).$

The asymptotic behaviour of the Whittaker functions follows immediately from that of the confluent hypergeometric functions. In particular we have

$$(17.28) \qquad W_{k,m}(z) \sim e^{-\frac{1}{2}z}\, z^k \sum_{j=0} \frac{(\frac{1}{2}-k+m)_j (\frac{1}{2}-k-m)_j}{j!} (-z)^{-j},$$

valid for $|\arg z| < \frac{3}{2}\pi$.

Integral representations of the Whittaker functions can be derived from (17.9) and (17.15). However, we mention the following variant of (17.9), the proof of which is straightforward:

$$(17.29) \qquad M_{k,m}(z) = 2^{2m}\, \Gamma(1+2m)\, \frac{z^{\frac{1}{2}-m}}{2\pi i} \int e^{\frac{1}{2}zs}\left(\frac{s-1}{s+1}\right)^k \frac{ds}{(s^2-1)^{m+\frac{1}{2}}} ,$$

where the contour starts at infinity with Re zs < 0, encircles -1 and +1 in the positive direction, and returns to infinity. A possible contour for the case Re z > 0 is sketched in fig. 17.1.

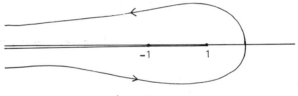

fig. 17.1

Confluent hypergeometric functions occur in a great number of applications. We end this chapter by considering as a typical case a Sturm-Liouville problem which occurs in the theory of viscous flow with a Poiseuille profile. The problem is to find the eigenfunctions and eigenvalues of

$$(17.30) \qquad \frac{1}{r}\frac{d}{dr}\left(r\frac{df}{dr}\right) + \lambda(1-r^2)f = 0 \qquad , \qquad 0 \le r \le 1,$$

where f is continuous at r = 0 and where f(1) = 0. Obviously this problem has positive real eigenvalues only and we write $\lambda = 4\omega^2$ ($\omega>0$). A simple substitution shows that the eigenfunctions are given by

$$(17.31) \qquad f = (2\omega r^2)^{-\frac{1}{2}} M_{\frac{1}{2}\omega,0}(2\omega r^2) = e^{-\omega r^2} M(\tfrac{1}{2}-\tfrac{1}{2}\omega,1,2\omega r^2).$$

110

It follows from (17.8) that also

$$(17.32) \qquad f = e^{\omega r^2} M(\tfrac{1}{2}+\tfrac{1}{2}\omega, 1, -2\omega r^2) ,$$

so that f is an even function of ω.
The eigenvalues are determined by

$$(17.33) \qquad M_{\tfrac{1}{2}\omega, 0}(2\omega) = 0.$$

The discussion of this problem for large ω requires asymptotic expansions of a similar kind as those in the preceding chapter.

From (17.29) and (17.31) we obtain the integral representation

$$(17.34) \qquad f = \frac{1}{2\pi i} \int^{(+1)} e^{\omega r^2 z} \left(\frac{z-1}{z+1}\right)^{\tfrac{1}{2}\omega} \frac{dz}{\sqrt{z^2-1}} .$$

This is of the form (11.1) with

$$(17.35) \qquad \phi(z) = -r^2 z + \tfrac{1}{2} \log \frac{z+1}{z-1} .$$

Writing $r = \sin \alpha$, $0 < \alpha \leq \tfrac{1}{2}\pi$, the saddle points are found from

$$\phi'(z) = -\sin^2\alpha + \frac{1}{1-z^2} = 0$$

as $z = \pm i \cot g \alpha$.
The corresponding lines of steepest descent are given by

$$(17.36) \qquad \sin^2\alpha \ \mathrm{Im} \ z -\tfrac{1}{2} \arg \frac{z+1}{z-1} = \pm (\sin \alpha \cos \alpha + \alpha).$$

They are sketched in fig. 17.2.

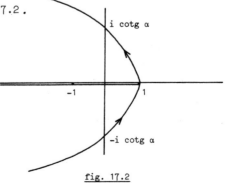

fig. 17.2

Since f is real, it suffices to take twice the real part of the contribution of the upper steepest descent path. There we make the substitution

(17.37) $\phi(z) = -i(\sin \alpha \cos \alpha + \alpha) + s^2.$

Locally at $z = i\cotg\,\alpha$ this means

(17.38) $z = i\cotg\,\alpha - i^{\frac{1}{2}}s\,\sin^{-3/2}\alpha\,\cos^{-\frac{1}{2}}\alpha + \ldots\,,$

so that at the saddle point the steepest descent path makes an angle of $\frac{1}{4}\pi$ with the imaginary axis. The contribution along this path is

(17.39) $\exp - i\omega(\sin \alpha \cos \alpha + \alpha)\,\dfrac{1}{2\pi i}\displaystyle\int_{-\infty}^{\infty} e^{-\omega s^2}\,(\dfrac{dz}{ds}\dfrac{1}{\sqrt{z^2-1}})ds.$

A simple calculation shows that

(17.40) $(z^2-1)^{-\frac{1}{2}}\dfrac{dz}{ds} = i^{3/2}\,\sin^{-\frac{1}{2}}\alpha\,\cos^{-\frac{1}{2}}\alpha + O(s).$

Higher terms can be calculated in the usual way. However, restricting ourselves to the leading term, we find eventually

(17.41)
$$f = e^{-r^2} M(\tfrac{1}{2}-\tfrac{1}{2}\omega,1,2\omega\,\sin^2\alpha) \sim$$
$$\sim (\pi\omega\,\sin \alpha\,\cos \alpha)^{-\frac{1}{2}}\,\cos(\omega(\sin \alpha \cos \alpha+\alpha) - \tfrac{1}{4}\pi).$$

As is to be expected, the AE breaks down at the endpoints. In order to discuss the eigenvalue equation (17.33) for large ω, we consider anew (17.34) with $r = 1$. There is a third order saddle point at the origin. The lines of steepest descent are now given by

(17.42) $\text{Im } z - \tfrac{1}{2}\arg\dfrac{z+1}{z-1} = \pm\,\tfrac{1}{2}\pi.$

They are sketched in figure 17.3.

112

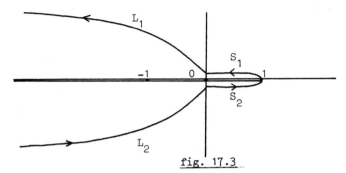

fig. 17.3

The combined path of integration consists of two lines in the second and
third quadrant with the equation

(17.43) $x^2 = 2y \cot 2y + 1 - y^2,$

where $z = x + iy$, and two segments on the positive real axis between 0 and
1 on both sides of the cut from $-\infty$ to 1. We make the transformation

(17.44) $- z + \tfrac{1}{2} \log \dfrac{1+z}{1-z} = s^3$

with $\arg s = 0$ for z on S_1 and S_2,

$\arg s = \dfrac{2}{3}\pi$ on L_1 and

$\arg s = - \dfrac{2}{3}\pi$ on L_2.

Again it suffices to consider the contributions of L_1 and S_1. This gives

(17.45)
$$f = \frac{1}{\pi} \operatorname{Re} \left\{ e^{\tfrac{1}{2}\pi\omega i} \int_0^\infty e^{-\omega s^3} \frac{dz}{ds} (1-z^2)^{-\tfrac{1}{2}} ds - e^{\tfrac{1}{2}\pi\omega i} \int_0^\infty \exp\tfrac{2}{3}\pi i \, e^{-\omega s^3} \frac{dz}{ds} (1-z^2)^{-\tfrac{1}{2}} ds \right\}.$$

From the expansion of $\dfrac{dz}{ds} (1-z^2)^{-\tfrac{1}{2}}$ in powers of s the AE of f is found in a
straightforward way.
Writing

(17.46) $\dfrac{dz}{ds} (1-z^2)^{-\tfrac{1}{2}} = \sum_{k=0}^{\infty} m_k s^k,$

we obtain

$$(17.47) \quad (2\omega)^{-\frac{1}{2}} M_{\frac{1}{2}\omega,\nu}(2\omega) \sim \frac{2}{3\pi} \sum_{k=0} m_k \ \Gamma(\tfrac{1}{3}k+\tfrac{1}{3}) \ \sin \tfrac{1}{3}(k+1)\pi \ .$$

$$. \ \sin (\tfrac{1}{2}\omega + \tfrac{1}{3}k + \tfrac{1}{3})\pi \ . \ \omega^{-\frac{1}{3}(k+1)} \ .$$

The first few values of m_k can be obtained from (17.46) by substituting the inverse expansion of z in powers of s,

$$z = 3^{1/3} \ s - \frac{3}{5}s^3 + \dots \ .$$

This gives

$$m_0 = 3^{1/3} \quad , \quad m_1 = 0 \quad , \quad m_2 = -\frac{3}{10} \quad , \quad m_3 = 0,$$

so that explicitly

$$(17.48) \quad (2\omega)^{-\frac{1}{2}} M_{\frac{1}{2}\omega,0}(2\omega) \sim \frac{1}{\pi} 3^{-1/6} \ \Gamma(\tfrac{1}{3})\omega^{-1/3} \ \sin (\tfrac{1}{2}\omega + \tfrac{1}{3})\pi + 0(\omega^{-4/3}).$$

For $\omega \to \infty$ the eigenvalues follow from $\sin (\tfrac{1}{2}\omega + \tfrac{1}{3})\pi = 0$ as

$$(17.49) \quad \omega_n = 2n + \frac{4}{3} \quad , \quad n \to \infty \ .$$

A numerical calculation of the lowest eigenvalues give

$$\omega_0 = 1.35 \quad , \quad \omega_1 = 3.34 \quad , \quad \dots \ .$$

Surprisingly the asymptotic estimate (17.49) is already quite good for the lowest possible values of n.

18. HERMITE FUNCTIONS

Although the Hermite functions may be considered as a special case of the confluent hypergeometric functions, they deserve a special treatment. We consider here in particular the asymptotic behaviour of the Hermite polynomials $He_n(x)$ for large values of x and n where x is real and positive.

The Hermite polynomials $He_n(x)$ may be defined by the following generating function

$$(18.1) \qquad \exp(-\tfrac{1}{2}t^2+xt) = \sum_{n=0}^{\infty} He_n(x) \frac{t^n}{n!} .$$

The first few polynomials are

$$He_0(x) = 1 \qquad\qquad He_3(x) = x^3 - 3x$$
$$He_1(x) = x \qquad\qquad He_4(x) = x^4 - 6x^2 + 3.$$
$$He_2(x) = x^2 - 1$$

From the coefficient formula of a Taylor expansion there follows at once the explicit integral representation

$$(18.2) \qquad He_n(x) = \frac{n!}{2\pi i} \oint e^{-\frac{1}{2}z^2+xz} z^{-n-1} \, dz.$$

An explicit expression for general n can be derived from this by expanding the integrand in powers of x and integrating the resulting series. A straightforward calculation shows that

$$He_{2m}(x) = \frac{(-1)^m (2m)!}{2^m \, m!} M(-m,\tfrac{1}{2},\tfrac{1}{2}x^2) ,$$

$$(18.3)$$

$$He_{2m+1}(x) = \frac{(-1)^m (2m+1)!}{2^m \, m!} x M(-m,\tfrac{3}{2},\tfrac{1}{2}x^2).$$

The Hermite polynomials defined by (18.1) have a number of interesting properties. They are orthogonal with respect to the weight function $\exp(-\tfrac{1}{2}x^2)$ and they satisfy the differential equation

$$(18.4) \qquad \frac{d^2f}{dx^2} - x \frac{df}{dx} + nf = 0.$$

Further they satisfy the functional equation

(18.5) $\qquad \frac{d}{dx} He_n(x) = n\ He_{n-1}(x).$

Sometimes the Hermite polynomials are introduced with respect to the weight function $\exp - x^2$. In order to avoid confusion, this second type of Hermite polynomial is denoted by $H_n(x)$. We then have

(18.6) $\qquad H_n(x) = 2^{\frac{1}{2}n}\ He_n(x\sqrt{2})$,

and in particular

$$H_0(x) = 1 \qquad\qquad\qquad H_3(x) = 8x^3 - 12x$$
$$H_1(x) = 2x \qquad\qquad\qquad H_4(x) = 16x^4 - 48x^2 + 12.$$
$$H_2(x) = 4x^2 - 2$$

The asymptotic behaviour of $He_n(x)$ for $x \to \infty$ is trivial since it is a polynomial of degree n. Of course

(18.7) $\qquad He_n(x) \sim x^n + 0(x^{n-2}).$

The behaviour of $He_n(x)$ when only n is large is more interesting. Starting from (18.2) we make the preliminary substitution $x \to z\sqrt{n}$. Then (18.2) becomes

(18.8) $\qquad He_n(x) = \frac{n!\ n^{-\frac{1}{2}n}}{2\pi i} \oint e^{-n(\frac{1}{2}z^2 + \log z)} z^{-1} \exp xz\sqrt{n}\ dz,$

an integral representation well suited for the application of the saddle point technique.
We find two saddle points $z = \pm\ i$ giving conjugate complex contributions. At $z = i$ we have

(18.9) $\qquad \frac{1}{2}z^2 + \log z = (-\frac{1}{2}+\frac{1}{2}\pi i) + (z-i)^2 + \ldots\ .$

The steepest descent curves through the saddle points which are given by

(18.10) $\qquad xy + \arg z = \pm\ \frac{1}{2}\pi \qquad , \qquad z = x + iy$, are sketched in fig. 18.1 .

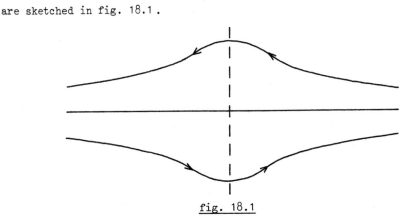

fig. 18.1

After the substitution

$$\tfrac{1}{2}z^2 + \log z = (-\tfrac{1}{2}+\tfrac{1}{2}\pi i) + s^2,$$

we obtain for the contribution of the path through $z = i$ the expression

$$- \frac{n!\; n^{-\frac{1}{2}n}\, e^{(\frac{1}{2}-\frac{1}{2}\pi i)n}}{2\pi i} \int_{-\infty}^{\infty} e^{-ns^2 + xz\sqrt{n}}\, z^{-1}\, dz,$$

where

$$z = i + s + O(s^2).$$

With due care of the term with $\sqrt{n}$, this can be written as

$$\mathbf{n}!\; n^{-\frac{1}{2}n}\, \frac{\exp\{(\tfrac{1}{2}-\tfrac{1}{2}\pi i)n+ix\sqrt{n}\}}{2\pi} \{ \int_{-\infty}^{\infty} e^{-ns^2 + x\sqrt{n}s}\, ds + O(n^{-1})\} =$$

$$= \frac{n!\; n^{-\frac{1}{2}n}\, \exp\{(\tfrac{1}{2}-\tfrac{1}{2}\pi i)n+ix\sqrt{n}+\tfrac{1}{4}x^2\}}{2(\pi n)^{\frac{1}{2}}} \{1+O(n^{-\frac{1}{2}})\}.$$

Thus, by taking twice the real part, we obtain at last

(18.11) $$\mathrm{He}_n(x) \sim \frac{n!\; e^{\frac{1}{2}n + \frac{1}{4}x^2}}{\pi^{\frac{1}{2}}\, n^{\frac{1}{2}n + \frac{1}{4}}} \cos(\tfrac{1}{2}n\pi - xn^{\frac{1}{2}}).$$

Next we turn to the more interesting case when both x and n are large. We shall write

(18.12) $x = 2\theta\sqrt{n}$,

where θ is a positive number. The expression (18.8) will now be written as

(18.13) $He_n(2\theta\sqrt{n}) = \dfrac{n! \; n^{-\frac{1}{2}n}}{2\pi i} \oint \exp - n(\tfrac{1}{2}z^2 - 2\theta z + \log z) \dfrac{dz}{z}$.

The saddle points follow from the quadratic equation

(18.14) $z^2 - 2\theta z + 1 = 0.$

Thus we may distinguish the following three cases

1. $0 < \theta < 1.$

Writing $\theta = \cos \alpha$ with $0 < \alpha < \tfrac{1}{2}\pi$ we find two saddle points $\exp \pm i\alpha$ on the unit circle.

2. $\theta > 1.$

Writing $\theta = \cosh \beta$ with $\beta > 0$ we find two saddle points $\exp \pm \beta$ on the real axis.

3. $\theta \sim 1.$

In this case there is a transition region with, for $\theta = 1$, a third order saddle-point at $z = 1$. It will turn out that the transition region can be adequately described by putting

(18.15) $x = 2n^{\frac{1}{2}} - \gamma n^{-1/6}$,

where γ is a real constant.

The three cases will be dealt with briefly. Details are left to the reader.

1. $\theta = \cos \alpha.$

The local behaviour at the upper saddle point is as follows

(18.16) $\frac{1}{2}z^2 - 2z \cos \alpha + \log z = \{(-\frac{1}{2}-\cos^2\alpha) +$

$+ i(-\sin \alpha \cos \alpha)\} + (1-e^{-2i\alpha})(z-e^{i\alpha})^2 + \ldots .$

Then for the leading term of the asymptotic expansion of $He_n(2\theta\sqrt{n})$ we find twice the real part of

$$- n! \; n^{-\frac{1}{2}n} \exp\{(\frac{1}{2}+\cos^2\alpha)n - i(\alpha-\sin \alpha \cos \alpha)n\}.$$

$$\cdot \frac{1}{2\pi i} \int_{-\infty}^{\infty} \exp\{-ns^2(1-e^{-2i\alpha})\}ds,$$

so that

$$He_n(2\theta\sqrt{n}) \sim \frac{n! \; n^{-\frac{1}{2}n} e^{(\frac{1}{2}+\cos^2\alpha)n}}{(2\pi n \sin \alpha)^{\frac{1}{2}}} \cos\{(\alpha-\sin \alpha \cos \alpha)n-\frac{1}{2}\alpha-\frac{1}{4}\pi\}.$$

Using Stirling's approximation, this may be written in the slightly simpler form

(18.17) $$He_n(2\theta\sqrt{n}) \sim \frac{n^{\frac{1}{2}n} e^{(-\frac{1}{2}+\cos^2\alpha)n}}{\sqrt{\sin \alpha}} \cos\{(\alpha-\sin \alpha \cos \alpha)n-\frac{1}{2}\alpha-\frac{1}{4}\pi\}.$$

2. $\theta = \cosh \beta.$

The complete steepest descent line through the saddle points is sketched in fig. 18.2 and given by the equation

(18.18) $xy - 2y \cosh \beta + \arg z = 0.$

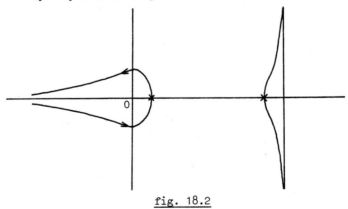

fig. 18.2

The asymptotic behaviour is determined by the saddle point exp - β only.
We have locally

(18.19) $\frac{1}{2}z^2 - 2z \cosh \beta + \log z = -(1+\beta+\frac{1}{2}e^{-2\beta}) - (e^{2\beta}-1)(z-e^{-\beta})^2 + \ldots$.

Therefore the leading term is

$$n! \; n^{-\frac{1}{2}n} \; \exp n(1+\beta+\frac{1}{2}e^{-2\beta}) \; \frac{1}{2\pi i} \int_{-i\infty}^{i\infty} \exp\{ns^2(e^{2\beta}-1)\}ds,$$

so that after elementary calculations

(18.20) $He_n(2\theta\sqrt{n}) \sim \frac{1}{2}n^{\frac{1}{2}n} \; \exp\{(\beta+\frac{1}{2}e^{-2\beta})n-\frac{1}{2}\beta\} \; \sinh^{-\frac{1}{2}}\beta.$

3. $\theta = 1 - \frac{1}{2}\gamma n^{-2/3}.$

Since the saddle point is situated at z = 1, it is advisable to change the
variable z in (18.13) into 1 + z. Then (18.13) becomes

(18.21) $He_n(2\theta\sqrt{n}) = n! \; n^{-\frac{1}{2}n} \; e^{(2\theta-\frac{1}{2})n} \; \frac{1}{2\pi i} \int^{(-1)+}$

$$\exp - (\gamma n^{1/3}z+ \frac{1}{3}nz^3+\ldots) \; \frac{dz}{1 + z} \; .$$

Using (15.8) we find at last for the leading term of the required expansion

(18.22) $He_n(2n^{\frac{1}{2}}-\gamma n^{-1/6}) \sim n! \; n^{-\frac{1}{2}n} \; e^{-\frac{1}{2}n \; + \; x\sqrt{n}} \; Ai(-\gamma).$

19. ASYMPTOTIC BEHAVIOUR OF CAUCHY INTEGRALS

We consider at first integrals of the type

$$(19.1) \qquad g(\omega) = \int_0^\infty \frac{f(t)}{t + \omega} dt,$$

where $f(t)$ belongs to a class such as $L^2(0,\infty)$. If ω is complex, $g(\omega)$ is easily seen to be holomorphic with a possible branch cut at the negative real axis. However, for reasons of simplicity ω is considered to be a positive real asymptotic variable.

The relation (19.1) can be written as a repeated Laplace transform

$$(19.2) \qquad g(\omega) = LL \ f(t).$$

According to theorem 6.4 the AE of $g(\omega)$ for $\omega \to \infty$ can be obtained from the AE of $\phi(s) = L \ f(t)$ for $s \to 0$.

Example 19.1

a. By direct integration we find that $f(t) = (t+1)^{-1}$ gives
$$g(\omega) = (\omega-1)^{-1} \log \omega.$$
b. Either by using (4.10), or by Laplace transformation we find for
$f(t) = \exp - t$ the result

$$g(\omega) = e^\omega \ \Gamma(0,\omega).$$

Example 19.2

The following results can be derived from a table of Laplace transforms

a. $$\int_0^\infty \frac{e^{-t} \ I_0(t)}{t + \omega} dt = e^\omega \ K_0(\omega) ,$$

b. $$\int_0^\infty \frac{J_0(2\sqrt{t})}{t + \omega} dt = 2K_0(2\sqrt{\omega}) ,$$

c. $$\int_0^\infty \frac{(t^2+2t)^{-\frac{1}{2}}}{t + \omega} dt = (\omega^2-2\omega)^{-\frac{1}{2}} \log(\omega-1+\sqrt{\omega^2-2\omega}).$$

If the Laplace transform $\phi(s)$ of $f(t)$ is explicitly known, its AE at $s = 0$ may be written down without difficulty. If, however, this is not the case or if $\phi(s)$ has a complicated structure, we may proceed as follows. Assuming that for $t \to \infty$ $f(t)$ admits the following APS

$$(19.3) \qquad f(t) \sim t^{\mu} \sum_{k=1} a_k t^{-k} \quad , \qquad 0 < \mu < 1 ,$$

we write

$$\phi(s) = a_1 \int_0^{\infty} e^{-st} t^{-1+\mu} \, dt + \int_0^{\infty} (f - a_1 t^{-1+\mu}) dt +$$

$$+ \int_0^{\infty} (e^{-st} - 1)(f - a_1 t^{-1+\mu}) dt =$$

$$= a_1 \Gamma(\mu) s^{-\mu} + a_2 \int_0^{\infty} (e^{-st} - 1) t^{-2+\mu} \, dt +$$

$$+ \int_0^{\infty} (f - a_1 t^{-1+\mu}) dt \; - \; s \int_0^{\infty} t(f - a_1 t^{-1+\mu} - a_2 t^{-2+\mu}) dt +$$

$$+ \int_0^{\infty} (e^{-st} - 1 + st)(f - a_1 t^{-1+\mu} - a_2 t^{-2+\mu}) dt \; .$$

Eventually this leads to the AE

$$(19.4) \qquad \phi(s) \sim \sum_{k=1} a_k \Gamma(\mu - k + 1) s^{k-\mu-1} + \sum_{k=1} (-1)^{k-1} b_k \frac{s^{k-1}}{(k-1)!} \; ,$$

where

$$(19.5) \qquad b_k = \int_0^{\infty} t^{k-1} (f - a_1 t^{-1+\mu} - \ldots - a_k t^{-k+\mu}) dt .$$

From theorem 6.4 we then obtain the AE

$$(19.6) \qquad g(\omega) \sim \frac{\pi}{\sin \mu\pi} \omega^{\mu} \sum_{k=1} a_k (-\omega)^{-k} - \sum_{k=1} b_k (-\omega)^{-k} \; .$$

The case $\mu = 0$ needs a separate discussion. Assuming

(19.7) $\qquad f(t) \sim \sum_k a_k t^{-k}$ $\qquad\qquad\qquad$ for $t \to \infty$,

we shall take the limit $\mu \to 0$ in (19.4) and (19.6). We note that

$$\Gamma(\mu-k+1) = \frac{(-1)^{k-1}}{(k-1)!}(\mu^{-1}+\psi(k)+o(1))$$

and

$$b_k = - a_k \mu^{-1} + c_k + o(1),$$

where

(19.8)
$$c_k = \int_1^\infty t^{k-1}(f-a_1 t^{-1}-a_2 t^{-2}-\ldots-a_k t^{-k})dt +$$
$$+ \int_0^1 t^{k-1}(f-a_1 t^{-1}-a_2 t^{-2}-\ldots-a_{k-1} t^{-k+1})dt.$$

Then we find

(19.9)
$$\phi(s) \sim \sum_{k=1} a_k(\psi(k)-\log s) \frac{(-s)^{k-1}}{(k-1)!} +$$
$$+ \sum_{k=1} c_k \frac{(-s)^{k-1}}{(k-1)!} ,$$

and next

(19.10) $\qquad g(\omega) \sim \sum_{k=1} a_k(-\omega)^k \log \omega - \sum_{k=1} c_k(-\omega)^{-k}.$

Of course the AE (19.10) can be obtained at once from (19.6). However, the expansion (19.9) is given here for its own interest.

More generally we may consider Cauchy integrals of the form

(19.11) $\qquad \Phi(z) = \int_L \frac{f(t)}{t-z}dt,$

where L is a path in the complex t-plane and $f(t)$ satisfies a Hölder condition on L.

By (19.11) a holomorphic function of z is defined in any connected region of the complex z-plane which does not contain L.

If $z = \infty$ is a regular point of $\Phi(z)$, which is the case when L does not extend to infinity, the AE of $\Phi(z)$ for $z \to \infty$ is already given by its Taylor series

(19.12) $$\Phi(z) = \sum_{k=1}^{\infty} (-z)^{-k} \int_L t^{k-1} f(t)dt.$$

A more interesting case occurs when L coincides with the real axis or with the positive or negative axis. If L is the negative real axis, (19.11) can be written in the form (19.1). Then $\Phi(z)$ is holomorphic for $|\arg z| < \pi$. At the negative real axis $\Phi(z)$ makes a jump which, after a well-known formula of Plemelj, can be described by

(19.13) $$\Phi(x+i0) - \Phi(x-i0) = 2\pi i \, f(x).$$

If $f(z)$ is an entire analytic function of z, the Cauchy integral may be written as

(19.14) $$\Phi(z) = f(z) \log z + h(z),$$

where also $h(z)$ is an entire function.

Example 19.3

The previous examples give illustrations of (19.14). In particular we obtain from example 19.1 a

$$\int_{-\infty}^{0} \frac{(1-t)^{-1}}{t - z} dt = (1-z)^{-1} \log z.$$

Returning to the representation (19.1) we note that the AE (19.6) and (19.10) can also be obtained in a direct way. The construction is here based upon the identity

$$\frac{1}{t + \omega} = \frac{1}{\omega} - \frac{t}{\omega(t+\omega)} .$$

Starting from the assumption (19.3), we may write

124

$$g(\omega) = a_1 \int_0^\infty \frac{t^{\mu-1}}{t+\omega}dt + \int_0^\infty (f-a_1 t^{\mu-1})\frac{dt}{t+\omega} =$$

$$= \frac{\pi}{\sin \mu\pi} a_1 \omega^{\mu-1} + b_1 \omega^{-1} - \omega^{-1}\int_0^\infty t(f-a_1 t^{\mu-1})\frac{dt}{t+\omega} .$$

Repetition of this construction gives the AE (19.6).

Example 19.4

It may be instructive to see what becomes of (19.6) in the case of example 19.2 a, where $f(t) = I_0(t) \exp - t$ has the well-known AE

$$f(t) \sim (2\pi t)^{-\frac{1}{2}} \sum_{k=0} \alpha_k t^{-k} ,$$

where
$$\alpha_k = \frac{(\frac{1}{2})_k (\frac{1}{2})_k}{2^k k!} .$$

The AE of $K_0(\omega)$ should be obtained in this way but it will turn out eventually that all coefficients b_k from (19.5) vanish. The reader may convince himself that this is true.

Example 19.5

For $f(t) = \exp - t$ all coefficients a_k vanish. However, (19.5) gives

$$b_k = \int_0^\infty e^{-t} t^{k-1} dt = (k-1)! .$$

Here we obtain the well-known result

$$g(\omega) \sim \sum_{k=0} (-1)^k k! \, \omega^{-k-1}.$$

20. THE METHOD OF THE STATIONARY PHASE

The asymptotic behaviour of integrals of the type

$$(20.1) \qquad f(\omega) = \int_a^b e^{i\omega\phi(t)} \psi(t) \, dt,$$

where $\phi(t)$ and $\psi(t)$ are real functions of the real variable t, can sometimes be determined in a relatively simple way by a method due originally
to Kelvin (1887). Kelvin states that the essential contributions to the
asymptotic behaviour come from neighbourhoods of the so-called critical
points, i.e. those points in a $\leq$ t $\leq$ b where the phase $\phi(t)$ is stationary.
In practice the method is used only in its simplest form for obtaining the
leading term of the asymptotic expansion. If, however, more terms are nee-
ded, the saddle point method is to be preferred.

Example 20.1

The asymptotic behaviour of the integral

$$f(\omega) = \int_{-\infty}^{\infty} e^{i\omega t^2} (1+t^2)^{-1} \, dt$$

depends on the behaviour of its integrand at the stationary point t = 0.
According to Kelvin we have the asymptotic relation

$$f(\omega) \sim \int_{-\infty}^{\infty} e^{i\omega t^2} \, dt = (1+i) \sqrt{\frac{\pi}{2\omega}} .$$

Since the integrand is analytic in the complex t-plane, an adaption to the
saddle point method is possible. If the line of integration is rotated
around the origin over an angle $\frac{1}{4}\pi$; we obtain the equivalent integral
representation

$$f(\omega) = e^{\frac{1}{4}i\pi} \int_{-\infty}^{\infty} e^{-\omega z^2} (1+iz^2)^{-1} \, dz.$$

The line of integration has now become a steepest descent path with a
saddle point at z = 0. Without difficulty we obtain the result

$$f(\omega) = e^{\frac{1}{4}i\pi} \sqrt{\frac{\pi}{\omega}} (1 - \frac{i}{2\omega} + 0(\omega^{-2})).$$

The following simple example shows the difficulties which may occur
when a saddle point method is not applicable, at least not in a direct
way.

Example 20.2

The asymptotic behaviour of the integral

$$f(\omega) = \int_{-1}^{1} e^{i\omega t^2} dt$$

is very similar to that of the integral of the previous example. The leading terms of the asymptotic expansions, depending only on the stationary
point t = 0, are identical. However, the next terms are different since
also the endpoints of the interval of integration contribute to the expansion. In fact we have

$$f(\omega) = \int_{0}^{1} e^{i\omega t} t^{-\frac{1}{2}} dt = \omega^{-\frac{1}{2}} \{ \int_{0}^{\infty} e^{it} t^{-\frac{1}{2}} dt - $$

$$ - \int_{\omega}^{\infty} e^{it} t^{-\frac{1}{2}} dt \} = e^{\frac{1}{4}i\pi} \sqrt{\frac{\pi}{\omega}} + i\omega^{-\frac{1}{2}} \int_{\omega}^{\infty} t^{-\frac{1}{2}} de^{it} = $$

$$ = e^{\frac{1}{4}i\pi} \sqrt{\frac{\pi}{\omega}} - \frac{i}{\omega} e^{i\omega} + 0(\omega^{-2}). $$

The first term is due to the stationary phase at t = 0. The remainder is
entirely due to the endpoints at t = ± 1.

We shall now give a theory of the general Fourier type expression
(20.1). For simplicity it will be assumed that $\phi(t)$ has a continuous second
derivative. Then the interval (a,b) can be split in subintervals where
$\phi'(t)$ has a fixed sign. The critical points determined by $\phi'(t) = 0$ can be
taken as endpoints. In this way the analysis may be reduced to that of a
few relatively simple cases. Before dealing with the general case we start
with a few well-known theorems.

Theorem 20.1 (Riemann-Lebesgue)

If $\psi(t)$ is integrable in the finite interval (a,b), then

$$(20.2) \qquad \int_{a}^{b} e^{i\omega t} \psi(t)dt \to 0 \qquad \text{for } \omega \to \pm \infty.$$

Theorem 20.2 (Dirichlet)

If $\psi(t)$ is integrable in the finite interval $(0,b)$ and of bounded variation in a neighbourhood of $t = 0$, then

$$(20.3) \qquad \int_0^b \frac{\sin \omega t}{t} \psi(t)dt \to \tfrac{1}{2}\pi \, \psi(+0) \quad \text{for } \omega \to + \infty.$$

Both theorems are well-known properties in the theory of Fourier series and Fourier integrals. It is not difficult to extend the theorems
for integrals with an infinite interval of integration. The result of
theorem 20.1 can be proved if $\psi(t)$ satisfies some smoothness condition.
In this way we have the following almost obvious statement.

Theorem 20.3

If $\psi(t)$ has an integrable derivative in the finite interval (a,b), then

$$(20.4) \qquad \int_a^b e^{i\omega t} \psi(t)dt = \frac{1}{i\omega} \{e^{i\omega b} \psi(b)-e^{i\omega a} \psi(a)\} + o(\omega^{-1}).$$

The improvement obtained here is due to the possibility of integration by parts which is such an important tool in asymptotics. The following theorem, which is a generalization of that of Dirichlet, is of fundamental importance for the theory of the method of the stationary phase.

Theorem 20.4

If $\psi(t)$ is of bounded variation in the finite interval $(0,b)$, then for
$\omega \to + \infty$

$$(20.5) \qquad \omega^\mu \int_0^b t^{-1+\mu} \sin \omega t \, \psi(t) \, dt \to \Gamma(\mu) \sin \tfrac{1}{2}\mu\pi \, \psi(+0)$$

with $-1 < \mu < 1$,

and

$$(20.6) \qquad \omega^\mu \int_0^b t^{-1+\mu} \cos \omega t \, \psi(t) \, dt \to \Gamma(\mu) \cos \tfrac{1}{2}\mu\pi \, \psi(+0)$$

with $0 < \mu < 1$.

Proof

We shall prove only the first statement. The proof of the second part is
very similar. In the first place we note that for the special case of a
constant ψ the theorem holds. Without loss of generality we may consider
next the case of a positive increasing function with $\psi(+0) = 0$. Applying
the second mean value theorem of integration, i.e. Bonnet's theorem, we
have for some mean value a

$$\omega^\mu \int_0^b t^{-1+\mu} \sin \omega t \; \psi(t) \; dt =$$

$$= \omega^\mu \; \psi(b) \int_a^b t^{-1+\mu} \sin \omega t \; dt =$$

$$= \psi(b) \int_{a\omega}^{b\omega} t^{-1+\mu} \sin t \; dt \to 0 \quad \text{for } \omega \to \infty .$$

We make the final remark that Dirichlet's theorem 20.2 is obtained by let-
ting $\mu \to 0$.

     We may turn now to the discussion of the method of the stationary
phase. We consider (20.1) where a is a critical point and b a finite ordinary point. More specifically we require that

(20.7)
$$\begin{cases} \phi'(a) = 0, \quad \phi'(t) > 0 \quad \text{for } a < t \le b, \\ \phi''(a) > 0. \end{cases}$$

Since $\phi(t)$ increases monotonously from $\phi(a)$ to $\phi(b)$, it is possible to
make the invertible transformation

(20.8) $x = \phi(t) - \phi(a).$

Near the stationary endpoint, a, this is of the form

(20.9) $x = \tfrac{1}{2}\phi''(a)(t-a)^2 + o\{(t-a)^2\}.$

Thus the inverse transformation is locally of the following kind

$$t = a + \left(\frac{2x}{\phi''(a)}\right)^{\frac{1}{2}} + o(x^{\frac{1}{2}}).$$

Substitution of the new variable into (20.1) gives

$$(20.10) \qquad f(\omega) = e^{i\omega\phi(a)} \int_0^{b_1} e^{i\omega x} \psi_1(x)dx,$$

where

$$(20.11) \qquad \psi_1(x) = \frac{dt}{dx} \psi\{t(x)\}.$$

For $x \to 0$ we have

$$(20.12) \qquad x^{\frac{1}{2}} \frac{dt}{dx} \to \{2\phi''(a)\}^{-\frac{1}{2}}, \quad \psi\{t(x)\} \to \psi(a).$$

If the last theorem is applied to (20.10) we obtain the result

$$(20.13) \qquad f(\omega) \sim (\frac{\pi}{2\omega\phi''(a)})^{\frac{1}{2}} e^{i\omega\phi(a) + \frac{1}{4}i\pi} \psi(a).$$

A similar result is obtained if $\phi(t)$ is a decreasing function such that $\phi'(t) \le 0$ and $\phi''(a) < 0$. Both results are summarized in the following theorem.

Theorem 20.5

If (20.1) has a critical point only at the lower endpoint such that $\phi(t)$ has a continuous second derivative with $\phi''(a) \ne 0$ and $\psi(t)$ is of bounded variation in a neighbourhood of a, then there exists the following asymptotic behaviour.

<u>a</u> If $\phi(t)$ is increasing, then

$$(20.14) \qquad \omega^{\frac{1}{2}} e^{-i\omega\phi(a)} f(\omega) \to (\frac{\pi}{2\phi''(a)})^{\frac{1}{2}} e^{\frac{1}{4}\pi i} \psi(a).$$

<u>b</u> If $\phi(t)$ is decreasing, then

$$(20.15) \qquad \omega^{\frac{1}{2}} e^{-i\omega\phi(a)} f(\omega) \to (\frac{\pi}{-2\phi''(a)})^{\frac{1}{2}} e^{-\frac{1}{4}\pi i} \psi(a).$$

Corollary

If $\phi(t)$ is either increasing or decreasing, we have

$$(20.16) \qquad \int_a^b \cos\{\omega\phi(t)\}\ \psi(t)dt \sim \left(\frac{\pi}{2\omega|\phi''(a)|}\right)^{\frac{1}{2}} \cos\{\omega\phi(a)+\tfrac{1}{4}\pi\}\ \psi(a).$$

If $\phi(t)$ is increasing, we have

$$(20.17) \qquad \int_a^b \sin\{\omega\phi(t)\}\ \psi(t)dt \sim \left(\frac{\pi}{2\omega\phi''(a)}\right)^{\frac{1}{2}} \sin\{\omega\phi(a)+\tfrac{1}{4}\pi\}\ \psi(a).$$

It is not difficult to formulate still more general theorems. However, in practice it is often more appropriate to subject a concrete problem to a more direct treatment along the lines indicated above than to apply some general theorem. This will be illustrated in the following two examples.

Example 20.3

Consider the integral

$$f(\omega) = \int_1^1 \exp i\omega(-t+2\sqrt{1+t})\ \psi(t)dt.$$

The interval of integration contains the inner stationary point $t = 0$. At this point we have the local expansion

$$\phi(t) = 2 - \tfrac{1}{4}t^2 + \ldots .$$

Thus we may apply the last theorem to the intervals $(-1,0)$ and $(0,1)$. In view of the local symmetry of $\phi(t)$ at $t = 0$ we obtain equal contributions from both intervals so that totally

$$f(\omega) \sim 2\sqrt{\tfrac{\pi}{\omega}}\ e^{-\tfrac{1}{4}\pi i}\ \psi(0).$$

Example 20.4

Consider the integral

$$f(\omega) = \int_0^\pi \cos\{\omega(t-\sin t)\}dt.$$

In this case there is a stationary phase at $t = 0$. Since, however, $\phi''(0) = 0$, we cannot apply theorem 20.5. Again we make the transformation

$$x = t - \sin t.$$

Near the critical endpoint we have

$$x = \frac{1}{6} t^3 - \frac{1}{120} t^5 + \ldots ,$$

and inversely

$$t = (6x)^{1/3} + \frac{1}{10} x + 0(x^{5/3}).$$

Substitution gives

$$f(\omega) = \int_0^\pi (2^{1/3} \, 3^{-2/3} \, x^{-2/3} + \frac{1}{10} + \ldots) \cos \omega x \, dx,$$

so that by applying theorem 20.4

$$f(\omega) = \Gamma(\frac{1}{3}) \, 2^{-2/3} \, 3^{-1/6} \, \omega^{-1/3} + 0(\omega^{-5/3}).$$

21. KELVIN'S SHIP-WAVE PATTERN

When a ship travels on a water surface it carries with it a pattern of bow and stern waves. The first mathematical explanation was given already in 1891 by Lord Kelvin (Sir W. Thomson). He showed by using his principle of stationary phase that the wave pattern caused by a moving pressure point was effectively confined within an angular region behind the disturbance of about $39°$.

We consider an infinitely deep sea $-\infty < x, y < \infty$, $0 < z < \infty$ where $z = 0$ represents the surface when at rest. The velocity of the flow is determined by the stream potential $\Phi(x,y,z,t)$ which satisfies the potential equation

$$(21.1) \qquad \frac{\partial^2 \Phi}{\partial x^2} + \frac{\partial^2 \Phi}{\partial y^2} + \frac{\partial^2 \Phi}{\partial z^2} = 0.$$

A disturbance causes a (small) elevation $\zeta(x,y,t)$ of the surface. We have accordingly the boundary condition

$$(21.2) \qquad \frac{\partial \zeta}{\partial t} = \frac{\partial \Phi}{\partial z} \text{ at } z = 0.$$

To this we have to add the equation of Bernoulli which gives a relation between Φ, ζ and the applied pressure $p(x,y,t)$. If for simplicity the density and the constant of gravity are taken as unity, we have

$$(21.3) \qquad -\frac{\partial \Phi}{\partial t} + \zeta + p = 0 \text{ at } z = 0.$$

The simplest model is furnished by taking a momentary pressure at $t = 0$ applied at the origin

$$(21.4) \qquad p = \delta(x,y)\, \delta(t).$$

This problem can be brought into a simpler form by applying the Laplace transformation

$$(21.5) \qquad \overline{\Phi}(x,y,z,s) = \int_{-\infty}^{\infty} e^{-st}\, \Phi(x,y,z,t)dt.$$

Of course $\overline{\Phi}$ satisfies also the potential equation. Using cylindrical coordinates r, θ, z, we note that $\overline{\Phi}$ depends only on r and z. The usual technique of separating the variables may give $\overline{\Phi}$ as a linear combination of solutions of the type $J_0(\lambda r) \exp - \lambda z$. Thus we put

(21.6) $\qquad \overline{\Phi}(r,z) = \displaystyle\int_0^\infty e^{-\lambda z}\, f(\lambda,s)\, J_0(\lambda r) d\lambda.$

A simple calculation shows that the boundary conditions (21.2) and (21.3) lead to the following relation

(21.7) $\qquad \displaystyle\int_0^\infty (s+\lambda/s)\, f(\lambda,s)\, J_0(\lambda r) d\lambda = \delta(x,y).$

From this integral equation $f(\lambda,s)$ can easily be obtained, e.g. by inverse Hankel transformation. We find

(21.8) $\qquad f(\lambda,s) = \dfrac{1}{2\pi}\ \dfrac{\lambda s}{s^2 + \lambda}.$

Substitution of this expression into (21.6) followed by inverse Laplace transformation leads eventually to

(21.9) $\qquad \Phi(r,z,t) = \dfrac{1}{2\pi} \displaystyle\int_0^\infty e^{-\lambda z}\, \cos(t\sqrt{\lambda})\, J_0(\lambda r)\lambda d\lambda.$

The elevation then becomes for $r > 0$

(21.10) $\qquad \zeta(r,t) = - \dfrac{1}{2\pi} \displaystyle\lim_{z\to 0} \int_0^\infty e^{-\lambda z}\, \sin(t\sqrt{\lambda})\, J_0(\lambda r)\lambda\sqrt{\lambda}\ d\lambda.$

We shall now construct an asymptotic approximation when both r and t are large. In this analysis only the leading terms of the asymptotic expansions will be written down. In the first place we use the asymptotic approximation

(21.11) $\qquad J_0(\lambda r) \sim (\dfrac{2}{\pi\lambda r})^{\frac{1}{2}} \cos(\lambda r - \tfrac{1}{4}\pi),$

which is obtained from (14.19) by taking the leading term.
Hence the product $\cos(t\sqrt{\lambda})\, J_0(\lambda r)$ in the integrand of (21.9) contains the oscillating factor

$$\cos(t\sqrt{\lambda})\, \cos(\lambda r - \tfrac{1}{4}\pi),$$

which can be written as the sum of two pure cosine terms

$$\{\cos(\lambda r + t\sqrt{\lambda - \tfrac{1}{4}\pi}) + \cos(\lambda r - t\sqrt{\lambda - \tfrac{1}{4}\pi})\}/2.$$

Thus the integral (21.9) is the sum of two integrals which can be treated by the method of the stationary phase. The first integral has no stationary point but the second integral has the stationary point $\lambda_0 = \tfrac{1}{4}t^2/r^2$. This means that only the second integral contributes to the leading term of the asymptotic expansion. Since

$$\lambda r - t\sqrt{\lambda} = -\frac{t^2}{4r} + \frac{r^3}{t^2}(\lambda - \lambda_0)^2 + \ldots,$$

we obtain by using (20.16) and (20.17)

$$(21.12) \qquad \Phi(r,z,t) \sim \frac{t^2}{4\pi r^3 \sqrt{2}} \cos \frac{t^2}{4r} e^{-\frac{t^2 z}{4r^2}},$$

and next

$$(21.13) \qquad \zeta(r,t) = \left.\frac{\partial \Phi}{\partial t}\right|_{z=0} \sim -\frac{t^3}{8\pi r^4 \sqrt{2}} \sin \frac{t^2}{4r}.$$

We consider next the model of a point source (ship) moving with a constant velocity c along the x-axis. If now the coordinate system is moving with the ship such that it finds itself always at the origin, the disturbance at (x,y), where x is fixed with respect to the ship, is given by

$$(21.14) \qquad w = \int_0^\infty \zeta(x + c\tau, y, \tau)\, d\tau$$

if the stationary state is reached. Putting

$$(21.15) \qquad x = -R\cos\theta, \quad y = R\sin\theta$$

where R is large, we obtain by integrating the asymptotic approximation (21.13)

$$w \sim - \frac{2^{-7/2}}{\pi} \int_0^\infty \tau^3 \{(x+c\tau)^2+y^2\}^{-2} \sin\{\tfrac{1}{4}\tau^2((x+c\tau)^2+y^2)^{-\tfrac{1}{2}}\}d\tau =$$

$$= - \frac{2^{-7/2}}{\pi} \int_0^\infty \tau^3 (1-2ct \cos \theta +c^2t^2)^{-2}.$$

$$\sin\{\tfrac{1}{4}Rt^2(1-2ct \cos \theta +c^2t^2)^{-\tfrac{1}{2}}\}dt.$$

The latter result can be treated again by the method of the stationary phase. There is a critical point for

$$\frac{d}{dt} \frac{t^2}{(1-2ct \cos \theta +c^2t^2)^{\tfrac{1}{2}}} = 0,$$

i.e. for

(21.16) $(ct)^2 - 3(ct) \cos \theta + 2 = 0.$

There are real roots only for $\cos \theta > \frac{2}{3} \sqrt{2}$ or equivalently $|\sin \theta| < \frac{1}{3}$. This means that only for the corresponding angular sector behind the ship the asymptotic behaviour is of the oscillatory type which is characteristic for the occurrence of a critical point in the interval of integration. Outside this sector the asymptotic behaviour is of an entirely different kind the discussion of which goes beyond the scope of this treatment.

136

22. ASYMPTOTICS IN THE THEORY OF PROBABILITY

In this section we give a few examples of the application of asymptotic expansions to the theory of probability.

We consider a sequence of n independent identical events. A single event is either a success with the probability p or a failure with the probability $q = 1 - p$. The probability $f(n,k)$ of exactly k successes in a sequence of n events is given by the well-known binomial distribution

$$(22.1) \qquad f(n,k) = \binom{n}{k} p^k q^{n-k}.$$

For n and k large this distribution tends to the normal distribution. This basic fact of the theory of probability will be derived here by means of the asymptotic techniques developed in the previous sections. It easily follows from (22.1) that the mean $\overline{k}$ and the variance s^2 are given by

$$(22.2) \qquad \overline{k} = \sum_{k=0}^{n} k \, f(n,k) = np,$$

and

$$(22.3) \qquad s^2 = \sum_{k=0}^{n} (k-\overline{k})^2 \, f(n,k) = npq.$$

It is therefore reasonable to introduce the new variable

$$(22.4) \qquad x = n^{-\frac{1}{2}} (k-np)$$

and to consider the asymptotic behaviour of $f(n,k)$ for $k = np + n^{\frac{1}{2}}x$. Applying the Cauchy expression for the coefficient of z^k in the expansion of $(pz+q)^n$, we have

$$(22.5) \qquad f(n,k) = \frac{1}{2\pi i} \oint \frac{(pz+q)^n}{z^{k+1}} \, dz.$$

This is of the form

$$(22.6) \qquad f(n,k) = \frac{1}{2\pi i} \oint e^{n\phi(z) - \sqrt{n}\,\psi(z)} \, z^{-1} \, dz,$$

with

(22.7) $\phi(z) = \log (pz+q) - p \log z, \ \psi(z) = x \log z.$

The condition $\phi'(z) = 0$ gives a single saddle point $z = 1$. In view of the local expansion

(22.8) $\phi(z) = \tfrac{1}{2}pq(z-1)^2 + \ldots \ ,$

we may introduce the new variable

(22.9) $z = 1 + it.$

Then

(22.10) $\phi(z) = -\tfrac{1}{2}pq \ t^2 + O(t^3), \ \psi(z) = ixt + O(t^2).$

With reference to the discussion of the chapters 10 and 11, the expression (22.6) can be written as

(22.11) $f(n,k) = \dfrac{1}{2\pi} \displaystyle\int_{-\infty}^{\infty} e^{-\tfrac{1}{2}pq \ t^2 n \ - \ ix \ t\sqrt{n}} \ F(t)dt,$

where

(22.12) $F(t) = (1+it)^{-1} \exp\{n(\phi+\tfrac{1}{2}pq \ t^2) - \sqrt{n} \ (\psi-ix \ t)\}.$

Since

(22.13) $- \tfrac{1}{2}pq \ t^2 n - ix \ t\sqrt{n} = - \tfrac{1}{2}pq(t\sqrt{n} + \dfrac{ix}{pq})^2 - \dfrac{x^2}{2pq} \ ,$

we perform the further substitution

(22.14) $pq \ t\sqrt{n} = - ix + u\sqrt{pq}.$

Then we find

(22.15) $f(n,k) = \dfrac{\exp(- \dfrac{x^2}{2pq})}{2\pi \ \sqrt{n} \ pq} \displaystyle\int_{-\infty}^{\infty} e^{-\tfrac{1}{2}u^2} F(\dfrac{u\sqrt{pq}-ix}{pq\sqrt{n}})du.$

There remains the technical detail of the expansion of the integrand function F of (22.15) in powers of $n^{-\tfrac{1}{2}}$. Of course only even powers of u have to be taken into account. We may as well take the real part of F only. It can easily be derived from (22.7), (22.9) and (22.12) that

$$(22.16) \qquad \mathrm{Re}\ F\left(\frac{u\sqrt{pq}-ix}{pq\sqrt{n}}\right) = 1 + \left(\frac{1+2p}{2pq}\ xu^2 + \frac{(1-2p)x^3-6pq\ x}{6p^2q^2}\right)n^{-\frac{1}{2}} + O(n^{-1}).$$

Then the required asymptotic expansion becomes

$$(22.17) \qquad f(n,k) = \frac{\exp\frac{-x^2}{2pq}}{(2\pi n\ pq)^{\frac{1}{2}}}\ \{1 + \frac{(1-2p)(x^3-3pq\ x)}{6p^2q^2\ n^{\frac{1}{2}}} + O(n^{-1})\}.$$

This shows clearly that for any fixed p and x the binomial distribution tends to the normal distribution. An inspection of the second term of the asymptotic expansion shows that the approximation by the leading term becomes bad if p or q is small or if $|x|$ is large. In the case of a symmetrical distribution, i.e. for $p = \frac{1}{2}$, the leading term is even correct within an order of $O(n^{-1})$.

Next we consider an application of a more general nature. Let x be a continuous stochastic variable with the probability distribution $f(x)$ such that the probability of finding x in the interval (x_0, x_0+dx) is given by $f(x_0)dx$. The sum S of n independent copies of x is a stochastic variable with the distribution

$$(22.18) \qquad g(x) = f(x) * f(x) * \ldots * f(x),$$

i.e. the n-fold convolution of $f(x)$. If $G(s)$ and $F(s)$ denote the (two-sided) Laplace transforms of $g(x)$ and $f(x)$, we have

$$(22.19) \qquad G(s) = \{F(s)\}^n,$$

so that in virtue of the inversion formula

$$(22.20) \qquad g(x) = \frac{1}{2\pi i}\int_L e^{xs}\ F^n(s)ds,$$

where L is a vertical path, usually the imaginary axis. The probability density of the mean $\overline{x} = S/n$ is then given by

$$(22.21) \qquad f_n(\overline{x}) = \frac{n}{2\pi i}\int_L \exp n\{\overline{x}s+\log F\}ds.$$

The determination of the asymptotic behaviour of $f(\bar{x})$ as $n \to \infty$ then proceeds in the usual way, e.g. by applying the saddle point technique.

Example 22.1

We consider the uniformly distributed stochastic variable x in the interval $(-1,1)$. The probability density is then given by $f(x) = \frac{1}{2}$ having s^{-1} sinh s as its Laplace transform. Formula (22.21) becomes

$$f_n(\bar{x}) = \frac{n}{2\pi i} \int_L e^{n\phi(s)} ds,$$

where

$$\phi(s) = \bar{x} s + \log \frac{\sinh s}{s}.$$

There appears to be a single real saddle point s_0 satisfying the transcendental equation

$$\bar{x} = \frac{1}{s_0} - \frac{\cosh s_0}{\sinh s_0}.$$

The local expansion at s_0 is

$$\phi(s) = \phi(s_0) + \frac{1}{2}(\frac{1}{s_0^2} - \frac{1}{\sinh^2 s_0})(s-s_0)^2 + \ldots .$$

Thus for L we may take the vertical path $s = s_0 + it$ $(-\infty < t < \infty)$ which at $s = s_0$ is tangent to the steepest descent line. If only the leading term of the asymptotic expansion is required, we have simply

$$f_n(\bar{x}) \sim \frac{n}{2\pi} e^{n\phi(s_0)} \int_{-\infty}^{\infty} \exp\{-\frac{nt^2}{2}(\frac{1}{s_0^2} - \frac{1}{\sinh^2 s_0})\} dt$$

or

$$f_n(\bar{x}) \sim \sqrt{\frac{n}{2\pi}} (s_0^{-1} e^{\bar{x}s_0} \sinh s_0)^n \frac{s_0 \sinh s_0}{\sqrt{\sinh^2 s_0 - s_0^2}}.$$

140

BIBLIOGRAPHY

Books

[1] Berg, L., *Asymptotische Darstellungen und Entwicklungen*. Deutscher
        Verl. d. Wiss., Berlin, 1968.

[2] de Bruijn, N.G., *Asymptotic Methods in Analysis*. North Holland Publ.
        Co., Amsterdam, 1958.

[3] Copson, E.T., *Asymptotic Expansions*. Cambridge Univ. Press, London
        and New York, 1965.

[4] Dingle, R.B., *Asymptotic Expansions: Their Derivation and Interpre-
        tation*. Academic Press, New York and London, 1973.

[5] Erdélyi, A., *Asymptotic Expansions*. Dover, New York, 1956.

[6] Hardy, G.H., *Divergent Series*. Oxford Univ. Press, London and
        New York, 1949.

[7] Olver, F.W.J., *Asymptotics and Special Functions*. Academic Press,
        New York and London, 1974.

[8] Milne-Thomson, L.M., *The calculus of finite differences*. MacMillan,
        London, 1951.

[9] Pittnauer, F., *Vorlesungen über asymptotische Reihen*. Springer,
        Berlin, 1972.

[10] Sirovich, L., *Techniques of asymptotic analysis*. Springer, Berlin,
        1971.

Papers

[11] Chester, C., Friedman, B. and Ursell, F., *An extension of the method
        of steepest descents*. Proc. Cambridge Philos. Soc., 53 (1957)
        599-611.

[12] Erdélyi, A., *General asymptotic expansions of Laplace integrals*.
        Arch. Rational Mech. Anal., 7 (1961) 1-20.

[13] Erdélyi, A. and Wyman, M., *The asymptotic evaluation of certain in-
        tegrals*. Arch. Rational Mech. Anal., 14 (1963) 217-260.

[14] Jones, D.S., *Asymptotic behavior of integrals*. SIAM Review, 14
         (1972) 286-317.

[15] Olver, F.W.J., *Some new asymptotic expansions for Bessel functions
         of large orders*. Proc. Cambridge Philos. Soc., 48 (1952)
         414-427.

[16] Olver, F.W.J., *Error bounds for the Laplace approximation for
         definite integrals*. J. Approx. Theory, 1 (1968) 293-313.

[17] Olver, F.W.J., *Why steepest descents?* SIAM Review, 12 (1970)
         228-247.

[18] Temme, N.M., *Numerical evaluation of functions arising from trans-
         formations of formal series*. Mathematical Centre Report TW
         134/72, Amsterdam, 1972.

[19] Waerden, B.L. van der, *On the method of saddle points*. Appl. Sci.
         Res. B, 2 (1950) 33-45.

[20] Wyman, M., *The method of Laplace*. Trans. Roy. Soc. Canada, 2 (1964)
         227-256.

[21] Wijngaarden, A. van, *A transformation of formal series*. Indag.
         Math., 15 (1953) 522-543.

CONVENTIONS, NOTATIONS, ABBREVIATIONS

ω   a positive variable, generally large

δ   a positive constant, generally small

z   a complex variable

x   a real variable

n, N   a natural number, generally large

k   an integer used as a summation index

AS   asymptotic sequence

APS   asymptotic power series

AE   asymptotic expansion

UAE   uniform asymptotic expansion

UAPS   uniform asymptotic power series

DE   differential equation

$$(\alpha)_n = \alpha(\alpha+1)(\alpha+2)\ldots(\alpha+n-1) \quad \text{for } n \geq 1, \quad (\alpha)_0 = 1.$$

INDEX

144

OTHER TITLES IN THE
SERIES MATHEMATICAL CENTRE TRACTS

A leaflet containing an order-form and abstracts of all publications mentioned below is available at the Mathematical Centre, 2e Boerhaavestraat 49, Amsterdam-1005, The Netherlands. Orders should be sent to the same address.

MCT 1   T. VAN DER WALT, *Fixed and almost fixed points*, 1963.

MCT 2   A.R. BLOEMENA, *Sampling from a graph*, 1964.

MCT 3   G. DE LEVE, *Generalized Markovian decision processes, part I: Model and method*, 1964.

MCT 4   G. DE LEVE, *Generalized Markovian decision processes, part II: Probabilistic background*, 1964.

MCT 5   G. DE LEVE, H.C. TIJMS & P.J. WEEDA, *Generalized Markovian decision processes, Applications*, 1970.

MCT 6   M.A. MAURICE, *Compact ordered spaces*, 1964.

MCT 7   W.R. VAN ZWET, *Convex transformations of random variables*, 1964.

MCT 8   J.A. ZONNEVELD, *Automatic numerical integration*, 1964.

MCT 9   P.C. BAAYEN, *Universal morphisms*, 1964.

MCT 10   E.M. DE JAGER, *Applications of distributions in mathematical physics*, 1964.

MCT 11   A.B. PAALMAN-DE MIRANDA, *Topological semigroups*, 1964.

MCT 12   J.A.TH.M. VAN BERCKEL, H. BRANDT CORSTIUS, R.J. MOKKEN & A. VAN WIJNGAARDEN, *Formal properties of newspaper Dutch*, 1965.

MCT 13   H.A. LAUWERIER, *Asymptotic expansions*, 1966, out of print; replaced by MCT 54.

MCT 14   H.A. LAUWERIER, *Calculus of variations in mathematical physics*, 1966.

MCT 15   R. DOORNBOS, *Slippage tests*, 1966.

MCT 16   J.W. DE BAKKER, *Formal definition of programming languages with an application to the definition of ALGOL 60*, 1967.

MCT 17   R.P. VAN DE RIET, *Formula manipulation in ALGOL 60, part 1*, 1968.

MCT 18   R.P. VAN DE RIET, *Formula manipulation in ALGOL 60, part 2*, 1968.

MCT 19   J. VAN DER SLOT, *Some properties related to compactness*, 1968.

MCT 20   P.J. VAN DER HOUWEN, *Finite difference methods for solving partial differential equations*, 1968.

MCT 21   E. WATTEL, *The compactness operator in set theory and topology*, 1968.

MCT 22   T.J. DEKKER, *ALGOL 60 procedures in numerical algebra, part 1*, 1968.

MCT 23   T.J. DEKKER & W. HOFFMANN, *ALGOL 60 procedures in numerical algebra, part 2*, 1968.

MCT 24   J.W. DE BAKKER, *Recursive procedures*, 1971.

MCT 25   E.R. PAERL, *Representations of the Lorentz group and projective geometry*, 1969.

MCT 26   EUROPEAN MEETING 1968, *Selected statistical papers, part I*, 1968.

MCT 27   EUROPEAN MEETING 1968, *Selected statistical papers, part II*, 1969.

MCT 28   J. OOSTERHOFF, *Combination of one-sided statistical tests*, 1969.

MCT 29   J. VERHOEFF, *Error detecting decimal codes*, 1969.

MCT 30 H. BRANDT CORSTIUS, *Excercises in computational linguistics*, 1970.

MCT 31 W. MOLENAAR, *Approximations to the Poisson, binomial and hypergeometric distribution functions*, 1970.

MCT 32 L. DE HAAN, *On regular variation and its application to the weak convergence of sample extremes*, 1970.

MCT 33 F.W. STEUTEL, *Preservation of infinite divisibility under mixing and related topics*, 1970.

MCT 34 I. JUHASZ a.o., *Cardinal functions in topology*, 1971.

MCT 35 M.H. VAN EMDEN, *An analysis of complexity*, 1971.

MCT 36 J. GRASMAN, *On the birth of boundary layers*, 1971.

MCT 37 G.A. BLAAUW a.o., *MC-25 Informatica Symposium*, 1971.

MCT 38 W.A. VERLOREN VAN THEMAAT, *Automatic analysis of Dutch compound words*, 1971.

MCT 39 H. BAVINCK, *Jacobi series and approximation*, 1972.

MCT 40 H.C. TIJMS, *Analysis of (s,S) inventory models*, 1972.

MCT 41 A. VERBEEK, *Superextensions of topological spaces*, 1972.

MCT 42 W. VERVAAT, *Success epochs in Bernoulli trials (with applications in number theory)*, 1972.

MCT 43 F.H. RUYMGAART, *Asymptotic theory of rank tests for independence*, 1973.

MCT 44 H. BART, *Meromorphic operator valued functions*, 1973.

MCT 45 A.A. BALKEMA, *Monotone transformations and limit laws*, 1973.

MCT 46 R.P. VAN DE RIET, *ABC ALGOL, A portable language for formula manipulation systems, part 1: The language*, 1973.

MCT 47 R.P. VAN DE RIET, *ABC ALGOL, A portable language for formula manipulation systems, part 2: The compiler*, 1973.

MCT 48 F.E.J. KRUSEMAN ARETZ, P.J.W. TEN HAGEN & H.L. OUDSHOORN, *An ALGOL 60 compiler in ALGOL 60, Text of the MC-compiler for the EL-X8*, 1973.

MCT 49 H. KOK, *Connected orderable spaces*, 1974.

* MCT 50 A. VAN WIJNGAARDEN, B.J. MAILLOUX, J.E.L. PECK, C.H.A. KOSTER, M. SINTZOFF, C.H. LINDSEY, L.G.L.T. MEERTENS & R.G. FISKER (eds.), *Revised report on the algorithmic language ALGOL 68*.

MCT 51 A. HORDIJK, *Dynamic programming and Markov potential theory*, 1974.

* MCT 52 P.C. BAAYEN (ed.), *Topological structures*.

MCT 53 M.J. FABER, *Metrizability in generalized ordered spaces*, 1974.

MCT 54 H.A. LAUWERIER, *Asymptotic analysis, part 1*.

MCT 55 M. HALL JR. & J.H. VAN LINT (eds.), *Combinatorics, part 1: Theory of designs, finite geometry and coding theory*.

MCT 56 M. HALL JR. & J.H. VAN LINT (eds.), *Combinatorics, part 2: Graph theory, foundations, partitions and combinatorial geometry*.

MCT 57 M. HALL JR. & J.H. VAN LINT (eds.), *Combinatorics, part 3: Combinatorial group theory*.

* MCT 58 W. ALBERS, *Asymptotic expansions and the deficiency concept in statistics*.

A star (*) before the number means "to appear".